Healthy Money

*Who's in control, you or your
money?*

Gerard Malone

www.advisordomain.com

ORIGINAL WRITING

978-1-906018-51-1

A CIP catalogue for this book is available from the National
Library.

Published by Original Writing Ltd., Dublin, 2008.
Printed by Cahills, Dublin.

Dedications

Where do I start? There are so many people to thank. This book is based on the study of a lifetime, and it is the result of having many mentors.

The first person to thank is my wife Mary for her patience, encouragement and endless enthusiasm. To our three children I say thank you; you have been fantastic with my working at home on this book and software.

My good friend Nancy Adams deserves lots of thanks for her smart editorial suggestions, and Paul Jackson for creating order and style out of my simple word documents. Paul has made this easy to read, he is a great editor. To the entire team at Original Writing, Andrew Delaney, Garrett Bonner and Steven Weekes for creating a wonderful hard copy version.

Abundant thanks to my great friend Christopher Johnson for his coding brilliance, patience, and for his great work ethic. You can see his work at www.advisordomain.com

You will meet people like the late Pat Howley and the late Tom Leacy who radically changed my life as a young man. Without them this book would not exist. To all the friends of Bill this book is for you.

CONTENTS

PART 2 Goals 76

PART 3 New Money Skills, get out of debt and prosper 137

PART 4 How To Master Your Mortgage   211

PART 5 The Keys To A Comfortable Retirement   230

Why did I?

Why did I write this book? Well it was based on learning from my own mistakes, accepting the wisdom of others and also learning what doesn't work.

Values are timeless and beliefs are changeable. I have tried to create a system that anyone can use. You do not need to share my religious beliefs nor do you need any religious beliefs to work this simple program.

When I left college I worked in financial services and since then I have had a varied career, as a writer, business owner, software developer and again as a financial advisor. What struck me coming back to the industry was how little had changed about our basic money beliefs. Many of these are false and you will see why I say this in this book.

Working as a financial advisor in New York City for the great Northwestern Mutual showed me that there is an abundance of help for the rich and not much for the rest of us.

Many of our beliefs about money were created to justify selling products, rather than products being created to match our beliefs. This is a small but vital difference.

I have been blessed to have started life with many privileges and to have also blown those privileges. I hope that this has made me a more compassionate person, better able to share my experiences with you.

My father the son of a banker was a golf champion and numbers wizard whose father died when he was only nine or ten and he was orphaned at twenty. This meant that he had to pass his exams as an accountant fast and he did so setting records in these exams that I believe lasted his lifetime. He had to take on the responsibility for being a parent to his younger siblings.

As a child many people would knock on our door asking my father for help as they knew he was an accountant. To these people he gave his help freely. Even though he was a numbers wizard you would have never known this as he had the common touch. So I learnt that what counts is simple language to explain how numbers affect our lives.

My other grandfather was the youngest of twenty one children. That must have not only been hard but mighty competitive. Eat up when the food is there or it's gone. He left school at an early age and in hindsight I would think that he had dyslexia. He grew up to be a successful and compassionate business man. At a time when memories of the civil war dominated Irish homes, he befriended many who were on the opposite side to him. Long, long after he died I found out that he gave a home to a widow with children. Her husband had died without life insurance and they were in great need of a home.

So how much credit can I claim for the good that is in my life? We are the product of all of those who have helped us and also those who have harmed us. I accept responsibility for my mistakes and I know that my successes have come from the help of many.

My goal is to give you a toolbox that you can use today. I want to change your life just as I changed my own. No matter where you stand today I am confident that you can improve your life with these tools.

I wish you every success in using this and I and I look forward to meeting you on the web to hear about your success and failures. One day there will be a worldwide community of likeminded users of healthy money skills. Together we will make constant improvements.

Yours in friendship,

Gerard Malone

PART ONE

AN INTRODUCTION TO THE BASICS

Everything that you master revolves around the basics.

With money it is learning simple tools, understanding certain truths and living by your own values. Beliefs are changeable, just look at our scientific beliefs! Values on the other hand are timeless. It is my opinion that many of our money beliefs are there because it suited people in the financial industry for us to hold those beliefs.

A simple example is that renting is dead money; well go tell that to a homeless person. This book while building on the strengths of those who went before me is also unique. For the first time we have a money book where you have a goal system that works. And the goals for you are not set by me. Typically in the world of financial advice we ask you questions so that we as advisors can set the goals.

I first learnt how to set goals while teaching in St. Gregory's school on the upper west side of Manhattan. This was a system designed by Cornell University. It had an amazing effect on children, and it will greatly improve your life if you use it. I have improved and added to the system over the years.

This money book is different. It works and you are in charge.

Your most important life changing money truth

▌ You either make money work for you or you will always work for money.

What makes healthy money so different from everything else?

I have a proven plan of action that works. It worked for me and everyday it works for people like you. When it comes to money you have only one choice to make. You either make money work for you or you will always work for money

You choose or by default someone else will choose for you!

- Diets don't work; if they did we would have no fat people. Money diets don't work. Diets are a short term fix. Anything can work for a short time. In my program you'll get no useless theory, no fluff, and no wordsmithing.

Wordsmiths paint beautiful pictures that sound great but when their plans are put under the spotlight they fall apart.

Tracking your spending will not change your financial life. You know that counting calories won't make you slimmer. Tracking can help as part of an overall program.

This program changed my life, and it will change your life. There is probably no mistake that you have made that I haven't made.

I worked as a financial advisor in NYC and studied what the rich Wall Streeters' did. I have observed people from every financial background and I have learnt just as much from them. Generally the rich can generate more income and they invest well, and they have a financial program.

To enjoy healthy money you need to be willing and to occasionally use a calculator. I have made the maths very simple to follow so that even if you have spent your entire life hating maths you will find this easy to follow.

This is a program to change your life not to sell you products. I am not trying to sell you a mortgage, a pension or any other investment. You will be able enjoy healthy money for the rest of your life and you will prosper by doing so. My goal is to help you become an informed consumer. This means that you will get a lot more from working with a financial planner. She will be able to help you pick the most appropriate products to accomplish your goals. This book is about using the principles, the products are the details. You need both.

All of the chapters are short, easy to read, easy to use and can be read in any order.

The worksheets work best in the order given. They are easy to fill out and the information from one is often used in another. You can fly through these, and do not worry about making mistakes. We are looking for progress and not perfection.

The goal worksheets will work for all areas of your life. This is a holistic program. There is no money side to you that is separate from the rest of your life.

- You can download free goal worksheets so that you can constantly change your goals, make upgrades, delete others that no longer inspire you and of course have multiple goals at one time that reflect your life.

This goal system is designed to work and not to shackle you with a list of mountains that you must climb. As your life changes so do your goals, and this system works under all conditions and for all ages.

Money affects every area of your life from work and in your personal relationships from the kitchen to the bedroom. No matter how good things are they only get better when you put your money to work.

You can go through the manual from start to finish or you can pick and choose.

I wish you every success in achieving financial freedom. I want to hear both your successes and suggestions. Soon we'll be a worldwide community of prosperous users of healthy money skills. Together we'll make improvements; you can help change many lives.

Yours in friendship,

Gerard Malone

2

Master this one life skill

▌ I want you to look at your life with a new set of eyes.
You must master lifestyle inflation

Look back on your life ten years ago. Your income today is probably bigger; you earn more and you spend more. This is the story
of my life as an income producing adult. As you go through
your life; this pattern will continue. This is good; it is the way we
are programmed to live. We work hard and in return we spend
more, we spend differently and we aim to enjoy more. We may
do this unconsciously but we still do it.

- **What separates your life today from ten years ago is
  lifestyle inflation.**

Lifestyle inflation happens when you buy bigger and better. Ten
years ago I enjoyed regular coffee now it is cappuccino. Ten years

ago a regular TV was good enough, today it is a widescreen. There will always be newer, bigger, better.

Look on your own life and you will see this creep in. If you want your healthy money to go further you will see the clues for saving money and yet still have a joy filled life.

The one skill that you need to master is lifestyle inflation. You can do this by getting emotional value for your money. I am not talking about being frugal; it is more about maximising your enjoyment.

Imagine that you are at a dinner party on a Saturday night. I am writing as a man, you can change the story to fit your circumstances. Sitting next to you is a woman in your age group. Her clothes hug her body in a sensual way, erotic yet not too revealing. You look at her face and she radiates confidence. Now you notice her hair, you can see it is an expensive hair style, elegant, attractive, it matches her face. Her eyes sparkle and her hair sits like a crown. From head to toe, she looks great.

To look this good this woman may have spent €300. It took €300 to turn up and look this good at a simple dinner party.

- Every woman has occasions like this. She'll take a lot of care and her close friends are wowed. She looks and feels great, special, and sexy. She is alive.

What type of man would say to a woman, you can't look this good, you can't feel this good? What the woman really wants are those feelings that I have described. For one woman €300 was an extravagance only for really special occasions, and for another woman it would take €3,000.

- I am only asking one simple question. What part has lifestyle inflation played in the cost of making you feel this good?

I know and respect your right to feel this good. You can look at your wardrobe with a new set of eyes. What you have spent, you have spent. For you there is no guilt, no recriminations.

If you're looking for ways to save you can start with lifestyle inflation.

Ok but how does lifestyle inflation affect everyone? If you don't understand this you will pay a very heavy penalty.

- It affects you when you retire, when it affects how long your money lasts.

Later in the book I will show you how to buy your retirement home when you're still working. The advantage you gain is that you can sell your existing home to boost your retirement savings. Or, you can rent your home for a monthly income.

I want to show you the affect of lifestyle inflation with these simple assumptions:

- Your home today is worth €300,000

- You spend €3,000 per month.

- If you sold your home today you would have enough cash to live for 100 months (300,000/3,000 = 100)

Time has passed and you're retiring. With normal inflation here is your situation:

- Your home is now worth €600,000

- Your €3,000 a month spending is now the same as €6,000. We are assuming that both real estate inflation and normal inflation grew at the same pace. This is unlikely but we will make this assumption for the sake of simplicity.

- Again, you could live on this cash for 100 months if you sold your home.

But this is the situation that you are more likely to face:

- Your income has increased.

- Your standard of living has improved.

- Because of lifestyle inflation where you are buying bigger and better you now spend €7,500 per month.

- This means that if you sell your home for €600,000 you can only live for 80 months. Divide 600,000 by 7,500 on your calculator and you get 80. Before lifestyle inflation you could have sold your home and lived on that money for 100 months.

This is a simple example. But it helps explain why you are making more money than ten years ago and yet you are not saving more.

A quick question for you; has your savings grown by at least as much as your income? For example, if your income doubled in the last ten years has your monthly savings doubled?

If you're honest you'll see that lifestyle inflation has crept into every area of your life. Later we'll use emotional value to maximise enjoyment for every Euro spent.

In the next chapter I am going to show you a new way to save. It is based on real life and not happy talk such as save ten percent of your income.

3

How to really save

One solution is to save a set percentage of your money. You've often heard the axiom save ten percent.

- This sounds good, but it doesn't work.
- It doesn't work when your income is low and it doesn't work when your income is higher.

This is why I disagree with a simple save ten per cent of your money axiom. This is a one size fits all assertion. You know that this isn't true in other areas of your life. Why should one size fits all be true in your savings arena?

When you are struggling to pay your bills, housing and food take a huge percentage of your take home money. When you are older and prospering you need to save more than ten percent. Why you might ask?

Good question, as your income grows and retirement comes closer you need to save a higher percentage ten percent won't cut it. You may need to save 15-25%.

So, you ask, where do I start?

- You start at the irreducible minimum. You save one percent. No matter how tight things are, you must find a way to save one percent.

As you succeed you will be able to improve.

As your income grows you can increase this percentage. One set percentage for all incomes is not smart. The lower your income the bigger your food and housing costs are relative to your income.

4

7 COMMON MONEY MYTHS THAT CAN HURT YOU

You can move forward when you can discard the nonsense that harms you. We have many myths that hold us back.We laugh at the notion that long ago people believed that the world is flat. A good myth is one that we can easily believe.

If you lost money by following any one of these myths you know this simple truth. No one will come to your home with money to replace what you lost.

1. *There is good debt and bad debt.*

You can invest all day long by borrowing but this doesn't make it good debt.

Ask any investor who has had a home or property repossessed by a lender. If you can't make the payments no lender wants to hear that this is good debt and therefore they should be more lenient with you.

Subconsciously we want to believe that if it's a good debt you must be a good person. Only good people get good debts, and bad things don't happen to good people, do they? Don't be naïve, there is no such thing as good debt. Invest all you want but don't call your debts good debt.

If you have borrowed for an investment, and that investment is held as collateral, the lender will call in that loan faster than lightning if you fall behind.

There are only two types of debt. There is only debt that you can afford and debt that you can't. Look at the downside, if it happens can you afford those payments?

This outrageous piece of nonsense has harmed tens of millions of families worldwide where people chased a piece of various bubbles. Invest in "appreciating assets" means you can't lose. Don't believe a word of this nonsense.

2. You can't lose money investing in real estate.

The answer to this is in number one.

In the late 1980's I saw clients lose real money investing in NYC real estate. Twenty years later I was at a wedding on the West coast of Ireland. Sitting at our table was a successful NYC real estate agent who told me you can't lose investing in NYC. The laws of investing (or bubbles) are different for NYC. It seems that every generation has to relearn the lessons of the previous generations.

3. Rents don't fall.

Study any free market and you will see that rents can rise as well as fall. If you had a hard time getting a tenant wouldn't you reduce the rent? Do you think that other investors are different?

3A. Renting is dead money.

This myth works like magic on first time buyers. It worked for me until one day I saw that the ultimate alternative was being homeless. You need a roof over your head. You can also do the math, and you'll see that there are many times in which it pays to rent.

4. You're too old to invest in a pension.

In an ideal world it's best to start young, but it's better to start today no matter what your age is. Sadly many people could but don't improve their retirement by saving even a little.

5. Don't prepay your mortgage, instead you take this money and invest to get a better return. Better yet they say "borrow more to invest more".

And then they show you pretty graphs with big numbers to back up this nonsense.

If the stock market tanks when you become unemployed how will you stand? What if property falls at the same time? Your granny told you, "When it rains it pours". Will your advisor guarantee that you'll make this money?

The myth here is that rich people invest rather than paying off a low interest loan. Take care of first things first. It's your home.

Lots of money is lost by people saying that I can't believe that this happened. Who could have forecast a perfect storm? When the money is lost remember it is your money that's lost. Invest all day long but keep this separate from your mortgage.

6. Pay off your highest interest loan first.

When you hear this it sounds great, intuitively you know that it is true. Sadly it isn't, not from the point of view of being debt free. It gets worse because it isn't true when you do the maths. Ok I was shocked when I ran the numbers for myself; I thought that it might be true. Our goal working together is to do what works.

7. Rich people make quick decisions.

You want to be rich don't you? This line is very popular by speakers selling in seminars. If you want to be rich do what the rich people do.

What these "gurus" never tell you is that Rich people can make quick decisions because they have seen so many deals. They know what they are looking for and they know if they have found it.

Think of the time when you met a person who looked good on paper but you could see through them. Rich people who invest can often have the same experience when they look at an investment. Being rich they can simply say straight out that this isn't for me.

- When you hear "do what the rich people do", follow this advice and do what the rich do most often and that is say no.

A rich person will look at one hundred deals, and say no to ninety nine and yes to only one! This is a pretty accurate assessment of what the rich people do.

5

COMMON SENSE FINANCIAL WISDOM

1. Money is a mood changer.

This is probably the most important fact to learn about money. I was in a van driving down Ninth Avenue in NYC with Dan. We were painting a small apartment building and we were behind schedule. Desperate to catch up we decided to rent a paint sprayer.

Dan turned to me and said "spending money is fun". The voice inside my head immediately contradicted him. Women enjoyed spending money we were spending money for work, this was different.

This simple comment helped change my relationship to money. I realised that men like spending money as much as women. We simply spend our money on different items. And both men and women enjoy the feeling, we change how we spend as we get older, but we still spend.

Think of how you feel when you get paid; think of how you feel when you get an unexpected windfall. Remember what it feels like to be broke. Can you remember what it felt like?

This is in my opinion why people borrow. It feels good to have the money, and borrowing is a lot easier than earning!

2. Before there was fast food obesity was rare.

When I was young meeting obese people was rare in Ireland, now it's common.

3. Before easy credit debt slavery was rare.

If nobody will lend you money, you cannot become overwhelmed with debts. As a business owner you can, but ultimately you still borrowed.

4. Minimum payments will eventually enslave you.

Minimum payments are fools gold. You pay less today so that the bank gets paid more tomorrow. Making minimum payments on a credit card means that you will never pay off the debt. You are simply making interest payments. As you pay down your balance you spend and so you borrow. To make things worse you are given even more money to borrow. This happens when the lender raises your limit.

5. Nothing but nothing costs only €xx per week. It costs €xx per week on top of everything else.

Payments that look small when viewed on their own will entrap you. Just 200 a month may seem small, but it is another 200 a month on top of all your other bills.

6. The worse your financial health is the meaner the lender.

When you are in a bad situation, a lender says we are taking a bigger risk by lending you money and for this risk we need to be paid more. Most lenders will look at your situation and say that it is irresponsible to lend you money. You are convinced that they are wrong. Into the breach comes the money lender. He will charge you usurious rates of interest, only the law will put a limit on his charges.

The money lender by the way thinks that he's providing a vital social service.

7. Nearly everyone thinks that they will make their payments. The reality is different.

Nobody borrows money thinking that I won't be able to make the payments. We all live in the land of wishful thinking. We all believe that it will all work out in the end. The lender also lives in the land of wishful thinking. They too think that it will all work out in the end. They think that the courts will work to get them all of their principal and all of their interest.

Sub prime was the greatest example of wishful thinking. Big powerful American banks felt that they could lend money to Americans who could never repay these loans. In turn the banks would sell on these loans to funds with small investors like Polish dentists. The banks believed that once they sold on the loan to the small dentist's pension fund that nothing bad would happen. And if it did the American Investment bank could wash its hands and literally say it was someone else's problem.

8. The sun doesn't always shine.

Before you invest or borrow you must learn this simple truth.

Your sure fire winner can in fact lose. You've borrowed because

your biggest client wants to buy more from you. Shortly after

you borrow your biggest client becomes bankrupt.

9. Diets don't work otherwise no one would be fat. Tracking your money doesn't change from being a spender to a saver.

Money is a tool not a way of life. I tried tracking for years. It

just did not work for me. It might work for you. Money like

food is part of your entire life; it is how you relate to money that

you need to change. When I eat bar of chocolate I'm probably

looking for an emotional need to be met. How you spend your

money is often done to fill an emotional need. If you are not

aware of this does not mean that this is not true.

10. When you pay more you don't always get more.

This was possibly the hardest lesson that I learnt in NYC. You

pay more and you do not get the best. There are many marketers who play on our fears and belief that if we pay more we get more. This is a way of life with information marketers.

11. *Any investment can fall in value. This means that you can lose money.*

You all agree but secretly you believe that when you invest you can only make money. Accept the fact that you can lose money and you'll be a more careful investor.

12. *90% of franchisees succeed is a lie.*

Once upon a time there was research done showing that franchisees succeed. This research is vastly out of date, and too generic to be of any value. I have met plenty of franchisees who have failed.

If you want to buy a franchise do vast amounts of research, including research on yourself. Are you suited to running this type of business?

13. The take away.

This is hugely popular with franchise sellers and so called marketing gurus. They say something like, we don't take everyone who applies, we are very strict as to who we sell to. You have to convince us that you are right for us.

We are closing this deal on Sunday, time is limited. In my experience these people all share one thing in common, they are dishonest. Your experience may be different from mine, if it is I would love to hear it.

14. If everybody is doing it, you are probably too late.

All bubbles end with this truth being relearnt for the first time by the many.

▌ You and your money:

15.   A person with money has more choices.

The more money you have the more people you can choose from. You can hire the best lawyers, the best accountants, the best financial planners. You will not have to borrow from a money lender.

16. *You alone are responsible for your life as an adult.*

You cannot change your childhood. For better or worse it will have left its mark on you. But as an adult you have the freedom and ability to create a whole new life that can be vastly different from what you have experienced up to now.

▌ Smart spending:

17. *Money back is not the same as time back.*

If you buy something that requires you to invest time to make it work for you, getting your money back is nice but getting your time back is impossible. Money back works for products but not for business opportunities or information sales.

Money back has a primary purpose and that is to increase sales. Most sellers know that even if you are unhappy you will not return the product.

18. *The longer the money back guarantee the less likely you are to return it.*

This follows from above. Sellers realized that if you lengthen the guarantee period the fewer returns they received. If you have only 30 days to return an item, you have this burned into your mind. If you have a year you are more relaxed. You can take your time to see if it works or to see if you got value for money. By the time a year is up you have forgotten all about it.

19. Look for weasel words in any guarantee.

An example would be; "Just show me you gave this program an honest to goodness try and I will refund all of your money, no questions asked". When you read the fine print this generally means that they have a thirteen point checklist that shows that you gave this "an honest to goodness try". If you only did twelve items you don't get your money.

20. Go with your instinct when you sense trouble.

Imagine walking down a dark city street and you sense danger. You change direction. Do the same with your money. If it sounds too good to be true it probably is.

I have saved so much money by not pursuing deals that just didn't feel right. I think that I have always been punished when I did not listen to my instinct.

21. "The numbers don't lie" is true.

Our difficulty is in understanding the numbers. Numbers are used to tell lies. Are you a numbers wizard? If the answer is no give numbers the same respect as a burning flame in your home.

22. Money problems can make you suicidal.

Right now as you read this someone is suicidal because of their money problems. This is why you must not only master the tools and techniques in this book but you must share this information with your friends.

▌ Making money is fun. It can make you as high as a kite.

23. If making money is more fun than sex, check your emotions.

24. Remember that money will not make you a better person, no matter what the sycophants say.

25. When you die those you worked with may forget all about you, your family will remember you forever. Make your memories good memories.

▋ Being poor is not a state of mind, it is a physical condition that can be changed!

There is a family I know and telling their story may help you. A boy leaves school at 14 and starts to work as a fisherman. A girl leaves school at 12 and starts work.

They travel across the water to work picking potatoes in Scotland. The farmer hoses down the cattle shed, puts some hay on the floor, and gives each worker a sack to sleep in.

At the age of 16, the boy lifts heavy rocks up from the beach and builds his mother a home. This was back breaking work.

Boy meets girl, they fall in love, marry, and have children. Life is hard, very hard, the husband has become a master fisherman and provides well. I saw a picture of that family when they were young and they looked poor, very poor. And if you asked them I think that they would have told you that they were poor. They will also tell you that hard work helped them have many material firsts in their area, the first phone, the first TV.

Now older and still in love they live in a beautiful home, and their children have moved away.

Here is what struck me about their children, they were all prosperous and some were wealthy. Most of you reading this would probably like to trade places in terms of money.

I'm curious and I wanted to know why they succeeded on such a level. The children now adults told me that their parents showed them how to work hard, the parents worked hard to make sure that they got an education; they were taught how to manage their money and to be generous.

A person, who says that I have been broke but never poor, could not possibly understand the magic of this true story.

They were poor and it is insulting not to admit this. Any child who travels across the ocean to work on a farm and sleep in the shed reserved for the cattle is poor.

Doing this back breaking work for 12 to 14 hours a day as a child was not an experience that any of us want our children to go through. But those who did could save enough money to last the long cold hard winter months back in Ireland.

This work broke many, and this has to be acknowledged. The point I am making is simple. You cannot judge a person by where they are standing today. Tomorrow we may be awed by where they stand.

The poor are not poor because of a moral failing; in my experience they are poor because of circumstances. We can change our circumstances and sometimes this can take a generation.

If you could go back in time and meet the heroes of our story, would you berate them for being poor? Would you call them a loser?

I think that they are one of life's great winners.

26. If you are poor acknowledge this.

There is nothing wrong in being poor; you are where you are. The problem starts when we stay poor. What direction are you going in?

27. When someone selling you a money making program says I've been broke but I've never been poor you are listening to a slick salesman who says borrow to buy my program.

Healthy Money Tip for Parents:

If you guarantee a loan for your child make the payments from your bank account. Your child pays you. This means that if your child cannot pay, you will make the payments. While this is painful your credit will not be destroyed.

When you guarantee a loan you are saying I will repay this loan if the borrower doesn't pay. Control the process and make the payments from your account.

If the loan payments are made from your child's bank account and they fall into arrears, your credit will most likely be harmed before you find out. This happens because the lender pursues your child first. There is often many months of arrears before they contact you.

6

WHEN IT COMES TO MONEY
AND RELATIONSHIPS ...

▌ Do men make the mistakes?

In personal finance the 80/20 Rule can be boiled down to one simple, painful fact;

When it comes to money men make the mistakes and women pick up the pieces.

Typically it was the man who borrowed the money, wishing, thinking, believing that it would all work out in the end.

Yes women do the same, and yes women can also destroy relationships with over spending. Under spending also harms relationships but it is a different type of harm. It is we can't spend because of our fears rather than we can't spend because the money is not there.

This is sad but true, and I have been as guilty if not more guilty than most men when it comes to making mistakes.

This book records how I accepted responsibility and picked up the pieces.

This book is your journey into true prosperity, enjoy the journey its fun.

7

NEVER MIND THE PRINTER, IT'S THE WOMAN

"Dad, dad come quick, we're not joking, it's really important".

As a parent I am sure you've had many of these "emergencies". These run from dad the ice cream van is in the neighbourhood to someone has fallen off his bike.

This one was truly different. One of our neighbours had a fire. Olga was a work at home professional. Like many of us she had built an office in her shed in the back of her garden. Now it was engulfed in flames.

David her partner was there, there was nothing he or anyone could do, the flames were too great, and we had to wait for the fire brigade.

I could hear David explain to another neighbour the expense of setting up the home office. They had just installed the latest and greatest printer for her architectural practice. "Thank God we're insured" he said. "We had to be covered. Olga will have to work from the living room until we can rebuild her office."

I was curious and I asked David what would have happened if Olga had been caught in the fire.

"What do you mean?" he asked, kind of appalled by my question.

My kids were looking on, eager to hear. "Well," I said, "if Olga had her hands damaged or her eyesight injured; how would she continue to work?" I asked him.

The two men David and his neighbour looked on me as if I was a fool.

"It's not the printer but the woman who generates the money. You've insured the things needed for the office, yes?" I asked.

"Everything in the office can be replaced, but Olga is irreplaceable. You need to insure her income. That is one of the lessons of today. The other is to be grateful that no one was harmed, and it's only your office and not your home that has been destroyed".

"Yes" David said while simultaneously making a phone call. I could hear him explain that he was ready to get that income insurance policy.

The truth is that many of us insure the printer, thinking that this is what prints the money bills. It's not; you are the machine that generates the money.

I made up this story so that I could ask you one question?

- Have you insured your ability to work from sickness or accident?

It is my experience that we will go to great lengths to work. Our industry or business may fall apart and we will seek a new way to make money. It is a sickness or accident that will stop you from working.

What stops one person from working may be an inconvenience to another. A cut hand may end a surgeon's career. What would prevent you from working? Call your financial advisor today and see what is available at a cost that you can afford.

8

A NEW START WITH HEALTHY MONEY SKILLS

In this book there is no filler. I have said what I wanted to say and nothing else. This means that you are getting pure content. This slim book is worth its' weight in gold if you give its simple tools and principles a try.

- What I am sharing with you works. Everything has been tried, tested and proven. Only then has it been given our seal of approval.

This book is about you, for you and not about me. It stands on its own two legs.

Our website www.advisordomain.com/forum will allow you to share your journey, both your successes and failures. Obviously I am so confident that you will achieve the same life changing success that we did. This is why you can share your journey on the open forums.

- *For the person who hates working with numbers rejoice!* You will be blown away by the simplicity and ease of use of these tools. As a former maths teacher I understand your fears. Relax and rejoice.

The entire maths has been turned and changed into "human math". Human math is all about using numbers with words to change your lives. These are numbers that anyone can use and understand.

I promise you there is no number exercise that you will have any problem with.

I know that some of you love words but you fear numbers. These exercises were created specifically with you in mind. Sometimes it is hard to look at where you are. If you want to change direction, you must know where you are. Every step is easy to take. You can go ahead and read the entire book before you do anything. Then pick and choose.

- How you manage your money affects every area of your life, from your work to friends, and from the kitchen to your bedroom. Money affects you emotionally, physically, spiritually and yes, sexually!

This book and program will change every area of your life. Try it you will see this for yourself. We wish you the same joy and success that we have had.

What you have in your hands is blending eternal wisdom, new ideas, timeless values with simple tools that combine to create life money skills for all ages.

Together, you and I, we are creating a worldwide revolution. Money will no longer be our God, but a tool, no different than a carpenters hammer. We will prosper and grow. Our economies will prosper and grow. *We will no longer worship at the false altar of indebted prosperity.*

Join with me today, and together we will climb this mountain. At the top, not only will we enjoy the beautiful views but we will leave a living legacy of prosperity for many generations to come.

My mothers' father, my grandfather left school at twelve. *One day when the local doctor died leaving his family destitute, my grandfather secretly gave them a beautiful home.* Today that home would cost millions.

Decades later, when I was in extraordinary financial pain, people came out of the woodwork to help me. Some of these people were strangers.

I honestly believe that it was my grandfathers' karma that caused this to happen. At the time I did not know what my grandfather had done. I only learnt this recently.

The good that you do today is like a ripple in the pond. Its effect may not be seen for generations to come. These ripples will be seen and felt and they too will create your legacy.

- What will future generations say about you?

Today you stand at the crossroads. Behind lies your past, and to some extent it's dead and buried. Let the dead bury the dead. Leave the past in the past where possible.

Move forward into a bright future and slowly but surely clean up the debris of the past. You can create a fantastic joy filled life that will bless many. Come join with me and create a legacy that will leave future generations gasping with awe.

You are living in the midst of the world's greatest renaissance. Now it is your choice. *What will your grandchildren say?*

9

WILL THIS PROGRAM REALLY IMPROVE MY MONEY LIFE?

Yes. Healthy money was designed and created for the person who knows that there has to be a better way to use your money.

Your desire to learn and your ability to use what works is so important. And, yes you can modify and change this program to custom fit your life. If you want to soar effortlessly like an eagle this program is for you.

To succeed you do not need to be genius nor do you need to have missionary zeal to use my recipe for financial freedom. This is a simple program that works.

- This is a fluid program of action.

You get suggestions, plans and tools that can easily be modified to your unique personality. No one like you had ever lived before, and no one will ever match you completely. When you

have children you see these small differences that are huge.
No matter how much you look the same or act the same, you
will never be your child and your child will never be you.

- The language of money is expressed in numbers. If
  you have always hated working with numbers relax,
  you can do every exercise with ease. We will be using
  human math, which is maths that anyone can use.

Why do I make this bold claim? The maths used is both complex and flawless, yet this is hidden from view. What you get are
exercises that will open your eyes to a better way of using your
money. We spend years in school and get almost no training
in how to manage our money. This is a national crime because
money problems are the number one cause of divorces.

What makes me so different is that I specialise in human
math. "Human math" are those numbers that when understood
by you they will change your financial life.

I taught maths in a New York primary school and the fear of
numbers is universal. My goal is not to elevate myself by claim-
ing to be a nerd. To do this I must make our relationship an
unequal one. I am forever the teacher and you are the student.

That is no way for consenting adults to behave. I know for a fact that there are many things that you can do that I can't.

This is a spiritual program of the best kind. It is rooted in earthly practicality. I am a religious man who prays every day. You may be an atheist, and here is our truth. There is no barrier between you and me; no barrier between you and our program.

From this point on my program becomes our program. As you use it, you own it. As you share healthy money with others, your ability to create joy in your financial life expands.

This program works. This program works with pen and paper. It works best with a computer because the calculations are done in a flash. This is why you should go to our site

www.advisordomain.com/book

10

TRACKING MONEY AND DIETS, MONEY MAKER OR MONEY BREAKER?

On a hot humid summer day in late August I was sitting down on the number 2 subway going downtown in NYC. Two men got on at 42nd Street. One of these men decided to hold court, as people sometimes do on the subway. I don't know if it is the free audience, the desire to be noticed or simply their desire to share their truths with the other passengers and get a conversation started. He was denigrating fat people.

In a loud voice he said "It's so simple, just eat less and exercise more. I mean come on what could be easier." There was no reason for anyone to be overweight. At this pronouncement he was happy.

I thought that this was absolute nonsense. I was 28 years old and honestly I did not have an ounce of fat on me, and I had never been overweight. And I had always assumed that I would go through life as a slim guy.

I was so annoyed at listening to this; it couldn't be that easy. My girlfriend and now wife was away in Ireland I decided that this was a good time to go on a diet. This was my chance to see what it was like to be on a diet. I went to Barnes and Nobles bought the current hot book on dieting and decided that I would follow it.

I cannot remember what the book was, but this is what I remember.

This was Monday evening, and I embarked on my diet. Included in this diet was the secret of healthy horses. They ate wheat grass and so I went as instructed to my local juice store and bought a wheat grass juice. Thank God this potent potion was small, it was disgusting.

- On Wednesday morning I quit the diet. I still think of this as being the worst three days of my life, despite the fact that it was at best 40 hours. I could not do anything but think about food, it felt like torture.

Can I tell you another horror dieting story?

Okay I give in, I will tell you. A client invited me out to dinner in midtown Manhattan. She was on a diet and ordered salad. This lady was very specific about how much salad was to come out on her plate, and when it was too little she sent it back for more.

Now my client takes out a small silver bowl from her handbag and starts to put the salad into it. The bowl is overflowing, so she crushes the salad down with her elbow. She continues to crush and add salad until the bowl can take no more.

"Why are you doing this?" I asked. She was on a diet and was allowed one bowl full. To me this was the opposite of freedom. This program is about money freedom.

Around this time I met some gurus who are famous for saying you should track every penny that you spend. Again I tried this.

- This is what I have found, tracking my money does not change how I spent the money, nor does it change how I spend my money. If you need to feel good and you go to Starbucks and buy an expensive coffee you will continue to do so. Only now you will feel bad. Tracking money only deals with the symptoms of overspending or under earning. Sometimes we need to look at the symptoms to see the problem, but tracking never worked for me.

What changes your life is having a burning desire to have a better life and learning the skills you need to do this.

If going to Starbucks is the highlight of your day why would you change this because you are tracking your money?

So I am against tracking, I think that it is a waste of time. I track my business expenses to the penny because the tax man pays me too. The more I can show the less tax I pay.

I accept that for many people tracking is an important tool, but I am not going to lie and tell you that I do it.

If you find anything in this healthy money program it is there because I use it and it works.

I do plan my important expenses, and you get the fixed expenses worksheets to help you do this.

If you want to change your financial life it is either earn more or change how you spend. Changing your spending habits is more important, because if you are overspending now you will overspend when you earn more.

A quick question for you;

As you look back over the last ten years are you saving more money today than you did ten years ago?

Changing your spending means I will not buy that latte today

because I really, really, want to have a starter emergency fund.

11

OVER SPENDING AND UNDER SPENDING

This is the only time that I really believe in tracking your money. You know yourself if your relationship is out of whack. Tracking your money will tell you where you are spending your money. Sometimes you need to see what you are not spending money on, as well as just how much you are spending on impulse items.

When you are going through difficult times in your life this will be reflected in your spending.
When you overspend in one area you will at the same time under spend in another.

- Spending money is one of life's great elixirs; it's up there with love.

Spending money is fun, and make sure that you understand this.

We get an emotional kick from spending money. Depending

on what we buy and how much we spend we expect a different emotional kick.

If I'm tired from overworking and I buy a coffee and mars bar I'm looking for a quick energy fix. I do it because I know that it works. If I go into a Starbucks and I buy a latte and muffin, I'm looking for a quick luxury fix. I want to feel like I'm winning at the game of life and that I can afford to spend extra because the truth is "I deserve it".

Spending like this is like drinking too much. It's great right now but the aftermath is terrible. This program will teach you how to give yourself a treat every day and it will make you feel great.

Everyone knows when they are overspending. The village idiot can look at an over spender's credit card statement and say you are overspending. It is harder to accept that you are under spending.

Okay so where could you be under spending?

- **Clothes.** When was the last time that you bought really good clothes that you were proud of?

- **Furniture.** Look at your furniture, are you proud of it?

- **Household furnishings.** Things like towels, bed sheets, kitchen ware.

- **Savings and investments.** If your spending is out of kilter how can you save let alone invest? Occasionally I will meet someone who over saves and does not spend money on themselves.

- **Education.** What if you invested in yourself rather than going out to expensive restaurants?

- **Your home.** You are living in a place that you dislike because you cannot afford to live somewhere better.

You can see that these areas are also the areas where you can destroy your financial life by overspending. You can be living in a great area but now you have no money to do the things that you love.

Our goal is simply to be aware of the choices that we make. We can change directions, and it as simple as getting off the bus and taking the next bus that goes in the opposite direction.

My experience has shown me that when I am making and living by right choices it is easier to avoid the impulse buy. Today when I go into a shop I ask myself "is this an impulse buy and can I afford it"?

If I can afford it I will probably buy it. Sometimes if I just ask myself is this buy an impulse buy is the brake that I need to stop. What happens is that I will admit to myself that I am tired and stressed out and I am looking for a break. If I can admit this to myself I can walk out of the store and not feel bad.

You can spend your money in any way that you see fit. I do want you to have clarity with your money. The road to financial ruin from Wall Street to Main Street is paved with financial vagueness. Money vagueness is a terminal illness.

The goal of healthy money is to have not just guilt free spending but enjoyable spending.

You can go to a financial boot camp if you want a strict rules based military style money program. My program is not for those people.

No one is going to "tut tut" you if you blew money in the mall instead of adding to your emergency fund.

My experience is that you blow less money, and have more fun by following this simple way of living. Under spending and over spending becomes a distant memory.

You will be free of hypnotic affirmations, free from nonsense like financial psychobabble. Nothing works like what works. Nothing changes your life like taking new and better actions. Change your actions first and then accelerate those changes with affirmations. As a man who prays regularly I believe that an ounce of action goes farther than a pound of prayer. Prayer works but not in a vacuum!

You are doing a lot of right things in your life. You record all the good in your gratitude journal.

Your goal is to get on the bus that is going in the direction that you want. If the bus moves slowly that's okay because you are moving in the right direction.

12

WHY DO YOU NEED AN EMERGENCY FUND?

Your reality is that you will go through life and face emergencies.

The only question is; how will you pay for these emergencies?

- *If you have cash you will pay for it with cash. If you have no cash you have no choice but to borrow the money.*

I drive a lot and on occasion my car will break down. The last time was a bank holiday weekend and the clutch cable broke. In the same week my wife needed a new exhaust for her car.

Without cash we would have to borrow. Most people use their credit card like a rich uncle. It is hopefully always there when you need it.

When we paid the €650 in car repairs we were finished with the ordeal. If we had borrowed we would have a financial hangover. Paying cash is so much easier, and the garage knows that we pay cash instantly. We are a priority client.

Everyone knows that you need an emergency fund but how do you do it? When we are told save 3 to 6 months this feels like an impossible mountain to climb.

It is the old joke; how do you eat an elephant? The answer is one bite at a time.

So the answer is to break your emergency fund into two parts, a starter fund of €1,000 and the balance at a later stage.

It is vitally important that this becomes your first accomplishment in our program.

What is the point of paying down your credit cards only to borrow again? It is your first act of financial freedom to start this fund. And yes it makes sense to do so even if you are being crushed by a credit card lender.

If you just pay down your balance and borrow for the emergency you'll feel defeated. You're back where you started, and it seems all the harder to go forward.

You will find that the act of saving will change your life if you have not done this before. When you are saving you are less likely to blow money on your credit card if you see the light at the end of the tunnel.

You now have the road map to your brighter financial future.

Many years ago in school we had a priest giving us a weekly sermon, he became stuck at "it is better" and then he couldn't finish his sentence, so I helped him. It is better **to light a candle than curse the darkness.**

- A starter emergency fund of €1,000 is how you light that candle.

13

HERE ARE 7 SIMPLE WAYS FOR YOU TO MAKE YOUR MONEY WORK

I am giving you seven simple tools that will change your life. They are so important that I could write a book around just these seven items. My goal is to help you change your life by presenting a lifetime of wisdom in the simplest manner.

Money affects every area of your life; these tools are help to help you be the master of your money. Today you may not be making a lot of money or you may be making a lot of money and yet you feel that you have nothing to show for it. This is how you change your destiny.

The universe is constantly changing, constantly growing. Your money life should be the same. We have an emotional relationship to money. When we change our actions we change our relationship with money. It is a fact that when you change your relationship to money you change every relationship in your life!

1. Pay yourself first.

No really pay yourself first.

This means that you save a portion every time you make some. The best way is to pick a percentage, such as 5%. This can grow as your income grows.

My question for you is this; have you paid yourself first? If your answer is no the time to start is today. Pick a percentage any percentage and stick to it for now. You can review this once a quarter.

You are where you are because of the actions that you have taken. If you change your actions you will change where you are. It's simple and it's true.

2. Your house payment is your most important payment.

The bigger it is the less freedom you have to spend money elsewhere. Your long term goal is to reduce your payment. The easiest way is to own your home free and clear, and I will show you how to do this.

3. Shop for groceries with a list.

You'll buy what you want and you'll spend less. You do this and the day will come when you don't need to do it.

4. Shop on a full stomach.

An army fights on a full stomach. When we're hungry we make bad decisions. When shopping this means we buy extra and spend more.

5. Think hard before you buy the best.

There is a time and place for everything. If you need your doctor for something basic you've wasted your money if you hire a surgeon. If you need brain surgery buy the best. If you need a standard will, go to a local lawyer who's reputable. If you are wealthy hire the best.

You would be amazed at how much money is squandered by hiring the best. You would be amazed at how many times you will be ripped off by people selling you on the idea that you need the best.

The pain of cheap work may be felt for a long time. For me the greatest pain has been in hiring people who promised great work and then didn't deliver.

Use your commonsense when spending. Get real emotional value for your money.

6. *It costs less to stay healthy than to recover your health.*

You live in and through your body. Treat yourself with respect. Drink water, go for a walk. There's no charge.

7. *Learn how to invest.*

In general a small business may be your best investment. This course is not all things to all people. Put first things first, save then invest.

You have just read seven simple tools that will change your life. Now put them into practice and take baby steps if you have to. These are easy to do, and they will bring more fun and re-move unnecessary stress from your life.

This is your life. As a young man I was told that the record only plays once. The older you get the more precious each day becomes. Go on, live your life to the max. Make the most of it starting from today.

Part Two

Goals

If you set and achieve your goals you control your destiny.

When you refuse to set goals you are letting someone else set your goals for you.

- So do you want to be master or servant of your destiny?

Many goals are killed at birth because you walk in two directions at the same time.

You want to save and at the same time you spend. You spend because you want to feel good or impress others. Whether you buy a Ferrari or a cup of coffee the principle is the same. It is the numbers that change but not the actions.

You want to become rich and you can't because you invest in the latest get rich quick scheme. It can be shares, bonds, real estate, and multi level marketing or even gold. The names change, but the scheme is the same, get rich quick.

Goal setting is a skill that you can learn. This is the one skill that you need to master if you want to prosper. All the worksheets you need are here, use them.

What you can accomplish with my system will astonish you. Come on, let's go.

GOALS MIND MAP

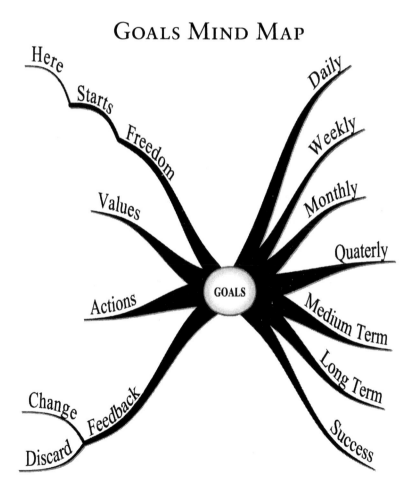

I

How does the goal system work?

This is a program for your entire life. Everything in here works. Your money affects every area of your life. Money is a mood changer and it is a hugely powerful influence on your emotions. Money is the number one issue in causing divorce.

A system for improving your financial life will only work if it is holistic. You start with your values, you use your talents, add time and you create accomplishments.

- *The difficulty is in having a simple system that shows you the way and allows you to custom fit for your unique life.*

The whole system is built on a spiritual approach to life and everything is built around Malone's law of the irreducible minimum. Everything in here is true, tried and tested. Everything works.

There are many tools that work for others such as tracking your income. I don't believe in this and you won't find it here. I discuss this later in the program and I will tell you when I know it will help you.

There is no magical hocus pocus, and no teacher student relationship. We are both adults. I am going to share with you what works and you can pick and choose. In this program we are equals.

I believe in simplicity, and you may prefer things to be complex. This program will work for you. This goal program will work for you even if every other goal program has failed for you.

- *This is a program about changing the direction of your life. You have probably done a huge amount of right things and we want to build on your strengths.*

If like me you work in a sales environment this system will blow you away. You will do more and get more done in less time. Give it a try.

Be patient the goal worksheets are the same but goals work best when interlinked.

I have been blessed to have had many mentors. One was the late; and for me; the great Pat Howley. Pat was a very simple man with great spiritual strength. When he was 50 he had to start over and in the process he helped change many lives, including my own. Pat told me two stories. The first was about a stubborn donkey.

The donkey refused to pull the cart and no one could persuade him. A widow owned the donkey and she needed him to work her small piece of land. One day she took the donkey to the local fair to see if anyone could help her. The widow was a pretty woman and there was no shortage of men willing to help. No one could succeed. At last a traveller came up, and they were much feared at the time.

"Let me try" said the traveller. He walked up to the donkey and gave him a mighty smack with his big stick.

"Oh my God what are you doing?" cried the widow.

"I'm just getting his attention" said the traveller.

After that the donkey did as he was told and the widow was able to till the land.

I always assumed that Pat told me this story because I was stubborn. Sometimes we all need to meet that traveller.

Another story that Pat told me was about the Second World War. In the British army the sergeant was going over the last minute instructions to the men going on their first parachute jump.

"Now remember", said the sergeant "pull the rip cord, but that is just a suggestion". I probably met or talked to Pat four to five days a week, and every day he told me this story. And I mean every day. Of course he had many wonderful suggestions which I still use.

This is a program filled with suggestions, which is why you have the freedom to pick and choose. The American army came up with a practical solution for their parachutists. They asked each person to pack his own parachute. It couldn't be any simpler could it? And it was hugely effective in saving lives from accidents.

So this program is a mixture of money skills and a flexible philosophy.

How do I use these goal worksheets?

- First of all I use them only because they work.

- I use them to create a much better life. Factually I have increased my income in a down market and I work less.

- This goal system has helped me write this book, create software tools for brokers, and come up with a solution for the housing and credit crisis. (Events overtook my solution. This was a solution to prevent some of the problems we now have at the time of printing).

Here are the 7 most important tips about using this program:

1. Print these worksheets.

2. Use them on a daily basis. They work best when interlinked.

3. Put them in a folder that you use every day. I have them in a folder with plastic sheets. This means that I can constantly see previous achievements.

4. In life just like in sports it is easier to win when you are already winning.

5. If they don't work for you, don't use them. But first try them and you will see for yourself this is the world's easiest goal setting system.

6. Some of these tools are emotional and spiritual. You may be uncomfortable with these but give them a try.

7. Contact me and share your success. I want to hear from you.

Do you want to accomplish any of these goals?

Do you want to be debt free?

If the answer is yes, start on a daily basis; get weekly feedback helping you accomplish monthly goals. Before you know it you are winning debt freedom in your first 90 days. This constant cycle helps you win and achieve your medium and long term goals.

Do you want to retire and live a comfortable lifestyle?

How can you do this if you don't have a Sat Nav for your hard working money. When you set goals on a regular basis you are less likely to chase the big deal. You are less likely to fall for the next hot investment which will give you wealth as a birthright.

Do you want to do more in less time?

An arrow flies best, and fastest, when it flies in a straight line. You are the same. When I set and track daily goals I do more, earn more and I am less distracted. It's fun.

Do you want to become wealthy?

Be your own company, by setting tasks, tracking what has been done, changing direction when you have to, and doing more of what is working. Change goals for tasks and you are on your way to hitting your prosperity milestones.

Have you tried to set goals and failed?

I have failed with many systems because they either did not deal with my personal values or they did not deal with the details.

Are you open minded?

Go on give the system a spin. You will be amazed at the results.

If you have ever taken a long journey by car, you can go back in your mind to that journey. Where were you going to? Where did you leave from? What was the weather like?

Were you driving?

Do you remember how without thinking you had a road-map for how you were to get there? Maybe you used a roadmap downloaded from the web, or maybe you got directions from a trusted friend, or you used a GPS, but when you started you had a good idea of how you would get there. Can you remember that as you travelled you monitored the petrol and oil gauges?

When you saw road signs for where you were going you unconsciously monitored the distance. First it was how far you had travelled from home and then it was how far you had to go.

All of this answered the universal question asked by children "how long to go"?

- This is no different from your new goal system, you have a goal, you are flexible when you have to be, you monitor your progress and you constantly evaluate.

When you arrived at your destination you were not surprised were you? Tired, cranky, elated but surprised? Go back in your mind to that journey when you arrived. Did you mentally calculate how long it took you? And did you compare this to how long you thought it would take?

This is why you will have tremendous success with my goal setting system. This system will feel like your favourite shoes. This is second nature to you.

No one else has put goals like this in a money program before.

When we set goals as financial advisors or writers we are always telling you what you should aim for. For the first time you are in charge. You decide what is important. You decide what you want to aim for. You know that this is true. Change your life for the better, and it all starts today, one day at a time.

Coaching Information:

I will be running 13 week (90 days) coaching group programs for anyone who wants to get on the fast track to goal accomplishment. You can go to our website www.advisordomain.com for more information. This will give you the bedrock on which to create the life of your dreams.

2

MALONE'S LAW OF THE IRREDUCIBLE MINIMUM

▓ Learn how to use this law and you can accomplish anything!

To accomplish any goal or task you can keep reducing what you need until you have the irreducible minimum. You are left with what you absolutely must have. This is the Law.

- You can accomplish anything with the irreducible minimum.

- Knowing and accepting this means that you can start from where you are.

- You are freed from the need to have all your ducks lined up.

- As you start to accomplish the tools and people that you need to do more will be attracted to you, but this is a side benefit.

- This law frees you from procrastination.

- This law frees you from needing everything to be perfect.

For example the law of the irreducible minimum states that if you want to write a love letter you only need a pen and paper.

This may sound both trite and obvious but this truth will help you accomplish many goals. In my business when I hire other consultants and providers they consistently tell me that if I want to do it right I must do it there way. They have been hired as the experts and so this seems to make sense.

What this really means is that they want me to take all the actions that Macys takes when opening a new store, when all I want to do is set up a mom and pop store. They tell me what's needed to build a skyscraper when I want a country cottage. So much time and money is lost by not using the law of the irreducible minimum.

Most of this book has been written with a pencil and loose sheets of paper. To get the first draft I did not need a computer, a thesaurus, a printer, no fancy software, no personal editor. Of course all of these were used later, but to accomplish my goal I just needed a pencil and paper. To print the first draft I did not need the new super duper printer that I wanted to buy. My old laser printer worked well.

I have been using the law of the irreducible minimum for two decades. It works.

To brush your teeth you need a toothbrush and toothpaste.

It is easy to complicate things; it's hard to keep it simple. Genius lies in simplicity. This law frees you from thinking that you must have more before you can do.

To start saving you do not need to wait until you get your next pay raise, you can redirect your spending and make a small start today.

Think about it, if you have never saved and you only save a few loose coins today, **you can now rename yourself as a saver.** *You are a saver and you are in the process of becoming a prosperous saver.*

Everything starts with using the law of the irreducible minimum. Your focus and drive can change as your life changes. As you begin to reach and accomplish one goal, this will change you and what you want to aim for.

What was important may become unimportant. What was once an unbelievable dream may now become your driving passion and your major life goal!

This program allows you to set and reach material goals. It gives you the freedom to grow and flourish as a spiritual being. Your goals are easier to accomplish when they match your inner desires. You will find it easier to reach your dreams when your short term goals are interlinked with your long term goals.

Goal setting is an integral part of your new relationship to money.

You are about to get a set of goal setting tools that you can customise to your circumstances. You decide where you want to go. You decide what is important. The set of tools that you are getting will help you sail through life, moving effortlessly with the wind at your back, and changing direction as you see fit

I was watching late night TV in NYC when I saw an ad for an anti gravity pen. You could write upside down and it had been invented by NASA for the astronauts who needed it. I like millions of others bought this pen. The Russians who were short on cash had a different solution for their astronauts. They used a pencil! This was the irreducible minimum in practice. How can you use this law?

3

CHUNK SIZED DAILY DO-ABLES CREATES SUCCESS.

Your life is lived in daily compartments. Today is the day in which you have fun for free and today you will accomplish more. Every step makes a brighter future.

This tool will make you a doer if you have struggled to make your dreams a reality.

Your daily do-ables are linked to your weekly goals. Your weekly goals are linked to your monthly goals, and these are linked to your 90 day goals. All lead to your achieving your long-term goals with ease and grace.

If some goals are wishes, put them on the shelf and leave them for another day.

Step one is to list your do-ables. Step two is to say who will do this.

Step three is your daily celebration. As you do each task acknowledge each victory. You are like a flower; you grow best in the sunlight of praise.

Example

What do you really want to accomplish today?	Who will do this?	Done?
1. Get Jones mortgage application sent online	Brendan	Yes
2. Tax Certs forms sent to clients who got €	Brendan	Yes
3. Approve new ad for Sunday	GM	Yes
4. Blog for brokers	GM	Yes
5. Insurance Quotes for recent mortgage applicants	Brendan	Yes
6. Pipeline follow up	Brendan	Yes
7. Create Survey real estate brokers	GM	Yes
8. Review next months marketing calendar	GM	No
9. Review website metrics	Jerry	Yes

Daily Do-able creates success

What do you really want to accomplish today?	Who will do this?	Done?

Source: Gerard Malone, for daily use you can download this form from our site.

4

WEEKLY GOALS

Linking goals helps you create better focus, and as a result, you will accomplish more in less time. Use this simple system and you'll be amazed at the results.

Your goal for this next week is something that you can actually accomplish.

Think of your goals as being links in a chain; it is strongest when all the links are joined. Your weekly goals strengthen when they move you closer to a long- term goal.

My long-term goal is:

Example
My long-term goal is:

Become Mortgage Free

You are an emotional person who uses logic as a tool to make things happen. It is your spiritual values that give true meaning to your life.

For this week's goal, choose something that you can do in the next 7 days.

My Goal for the next 7 days is:

>

Example:
My Goal for the next 7 days is:

> Count coins and make pre payment on mortgage.

What are your emotional reasons for reaching this goal?

I prefer to focus on the positive reasons; some of you will be motivated more by avoiding the negatives. Your reasons can be factual, legal, emotional, spiritual or physical. Emotional reasons work best for me. What works best for you?

Example:

What are your emotional reasons for reaching this goal?

This will be our third pre payment this year. It always feels great, being mortgage free will give us economic freedom. I will work from choice rather than need. We will have the freedom to live in different countries. Teaching kids by our example.

As you can see this is very simple, no PhD thesis, just easy to do action steps.

We are motivated by the thrill of winning or by the fear of losing. The emotion and its intensity can vary from goal to goal. I am motivated by the thrill of winning.

Include all of the positives or negatives for your goal. Why do you want to do this? You can be factual, legal, emotional, or spiritual. I prefer to focus on the positives; many are motivated more by avoiding the negatives. What works best for you?

I want to achieve this goal because:

| |
| |
| |
| |
| |

Weekly Goals

Linking goals helps you create better focus, and as a result, you will accomplish more in less time. Use this simple system and you'll be amazed at the results.

Your goal for this next week is something that you can actually accomplish.

Think of your goals as being links, a chain is strongest when all the links are joined. Your weekly goals strengthen when they move you closer to a long- term goal.

My long-term goal is:

_____

You are an emotional person who uses logic as a tool to make things happen.

For this week's goal, choose something that you can do in the next 7 days.

My Goal for the next 7 days is:

What are your emotional reasons for reaching this goal?

We are motivated by the thrill of winning or by the fear of losing. What works best for you?

Why do you want to accomplish this goal?

I want to achieve this goal because:

5

MONTHLY GOALS

Linking goals helps you create better focus, and as a result, you will accomplish more in less time. Use this simple system and you will be amazed at the results.

Your goal for this next month is something that you can actually accomplish.

Think of your goals as being links in a chain; it is strongest when all the links are joined. Your monthly goals strengthen when they move you closer to a long- term goal.

My long-term goal is:

```
┌─────────────────────────────────────────────┐
│                                             │
│                                             │
└─────────────────────────────────────────────┘
```

Example:
My long-term goal is:

```
┌─────────────────────────────────────────────┐
│              Become Mortgage Free            │
└─────────────────────────────────────────────┘
```

You are an emotional person who uses logic as a tool to make things happen. It is your spiritual values that give true meaning to your life.

For this month's goal, choose something that you can do in the next 30 days.

My Goal for the next month is:

```
┌─────────────────────────────────────────────────┐
│                                                   │
│                                                   │
└─────────────────────────────────────────────────┘
```

Example:
My Goal for the next month is:

```
┌─────────────────────────────────────────────────┐
│    Create a new software tool for my coaching clients. │
└─────────────────────────────────────────────────┘
```

Include all of the positives or negatives for your goal. Why do you want to do this? You can be factual, legal, emotional, or spiritual. I prefer to focus on the positives; many are motivated more by avoiding the negatives. What works best for you?

Example:

What is your emotional reason for this goal?

For example: I love the thrill of creating something from an idea in my mind to becoming a tangible product. I know that clients will love this tool. "I am a dreamer who does". Every time that I create a new product I am enhanced, engaged and a true participant in the game of life.

I know that I can create an extra income of €900 per month.

As you can see a small additional income can radically change your life. You do not have to pursue the big deal to make radical changes.

My own experience has been that every time that I create a new product it becomes easier to create another. I learn from the wins and losses.

Can you do something similar in your life?

We are motivated by the thrill of winning or by the fear of losing. The emotion and its intensity can vary from goal to goal. I am motivated by the thrill of winning.

Include all of the positives or negatives for your goal. Why do you want to do this? You can be factual, legal, emotional, or spiritual. I prefer to focus on the positives; many are motivated more by avoiding the negatives. What works best for you?

I want to achieve this goal because:

MONTHLY GOALS

Linking goals helps you create better focus, and you achieve more in less time.

Your goal for this next month is something that you can actually accomplish.

Think of your goals as being links in a chain; it is strongest when all the links are joined. Your monthly goals strengthen when they move you closer to a long- term goal.

My long-term goal is:

```
┌──────────────────────────────────────────────────┐
│                                                    │
│                                                    │
└──────────────────────────────────────────────────┘
```

You are an emotional person who uses logic as a tool to make things happen. It is your spiritual values that give true meaning to your life.

For this month's goal, choose something that you can do in the next 30 days.

My Goal for the next month is:

```
┌──────────────────────────────────────────────────┐
│                                                    │
│                                                    │
└──────────────────────────────────────────────────┘
```

What are your emotional reasons for reaching this goal?

You are motivated by the thrill of winning or by the fear of losing. What works best for you? Your emotion and its intensity can vary from goal to goal.

Include all of the positive or negative reasons for this goal. Be specific.

I want to achieve this goal because:

6

90 Day Goals

Linking goals helps you create better focus, and as a result, you will accomplish more in less time. Use this simple system and you'll be amazed at the results. Your goal for this next 90 days is something that you can actually accomplish.

You may prefer to call this your quarterly goal. I prefer to call it a 90 day goal because I can visualize taking a small action towards this goal each day for 90 days.

Think of your goals as being links in a chain; it is strongest when all the links are joined. Your 90 day goals strengthen when they move you closer to a long- term goal.

My long-term goal is:

Example:
My long-term goal is:

> Become Mortgage Free

You are an emotional person who uses logic as a tool to make things happen. It is your spiritual values that give true meaning to your life.

For this quarterly goal, choose something that you can do in the next 90 days.

My Goal for the next 90 days is:

>

Example
My Goal for the next 90 days is:

> Pay one month extra payment on the variable part of my mortgage. (My mortgage is split between variable and fixed. This insulates my family from interest rate increases. It also makes it easier to pre pay).

What are your emotional reasons for reaching this goal?

You are motivated by the thrill of winning or by the fear of losing. The emotion and its intensity can vary from goal to goal.

I am motivated by the thrill of winning. This is why I prefer to focus on the positive reasons; many are motivated more by avoiding the negatives. What works best for you?

Your reasons can be factual, legal, emotional, spiritual or physical.

Include all of the positives or negatives for your goal. Why do you want to do this? You can be factual, legal, emotional, or spiritual. I prefer to focus on the positives; many are motivated more by avoiding the negatives. What works best for you?

I want to achieve this goal because:

Example:
I want to achieve this goal because:

I know that I can accomplish this goal.

This is such a simple goal.

I know that this small step taken many times means that I am on track to reduce my mortgage term by 10 years.

(This is the specific goal that I have.)

You can download more of these goal worksheets at www.advisordomain.com/book

90 Day Goals

Linking your goals creates better focus, and you achieve more in less time.

Your goal for this next 90 days is something that you can actually accomplish.

You may prefer to call this your quarterly goal. I prefer to call it a 90 day goal because I can visualize taking a small action towards this goal each day for 90 days.

Think of your goals as links in a chain; it is strongest when all of the links are joined. Your weekly goals strengthen when they move you closer to a long- term goal.

My long-term goal is:

┌───┐
│   │
│   │
└───┘

You are an emotional person who uses logic as a tool to make things happen.

For this quarterly goal, choose something that you **can do** in the next 90 days.

My Goal for the next 90 days is:

┌───┐
│   │
│   │
└───┘

What are your emotional reasons for reaching this goal?

You are motivated by the thrill of winning or by the fear of losing. What works best for you? Your emotion and its intensity can vary from goal to goal.

Include all of the positive or negative reasons for this goal. Be specific.

I want to achieve this goal because:

7

MEDIUM TERM GOALS

Linking goals helps you create better focus, and as a result, you will accomplish more in less time. Use this simple system and you will be amazed at the results.

Your medium term goal is something you can do in the next 6 months to 3 years.

You use your goal chain to accomplish this. You use daily goals to help you reach your weekly goals. Your weekly goals break down your monthly goal into smaller doable chunks. Your monthly goals help you reach your quarterly goals. Now you have these bigger stepping stones to help you reach your medium term goals.

What you want to do is reach your goals. This is important if you are to create financial freedom. You can modify, change, and drop goals as you move forward.

Think of your goals as being links in a chain; it is strongest when all the links are joined. Your weekly goals strengthen when they move you closer to a long- term goal.

My long-term goal is:

Example:
My long-term goal is:

Become mortgage free.

You are an emotional person who uses logic as a tool to make things happen. It is your spiritual values that give true meaning to your life.

For this goal, choose something that you can do in the next 6 months to 3 years.

My Goal for the medium term is:

My Goal for the medium term is (in the next six months):

> Pay two months extra payments on the variable part of my mortgage. (My mortgage is split between variable and fixed. This insulates my family from interest rate increases. It also makes it easier to pre pay)

What are your emotional reasons for reaching this goal?

You are motivated by the thrill of winning or by the fear of losing. The emotion and its intensity can vary from goal to goal. I am motivated by the thrill of winning. This is why I prefer to focus on the positives; many are motivated more by avoiding the negatives. What works best for you?

Your reasons can be factual, legal, emotional, spiritual or physical.

Include all of the positives or negatives for your goal. Why do you want to do this? You can be factual, legal, emotional, or spiritual. I prefer to focus on the positives; many are motivated more by avoiding the negatives. What works best for you?

I want to achieve this goal because:

Example:
I want to achieve this goal because:

- I know that I can accomplish this goal. This is such a simple goal.
- I know that this small step taken many times means that I am on track to reduce my mortgage term by 10 years. (This is the specific goal that I have.)

MEDIUM TERM GOALS

Linking your goals creates better focus, and you achieve more in less time.

Your medium term goal is something you **can do** in the next 6 months to 3 years.

You will use your goal chain to accomplish this. You are using daily goals to help you reach your weekly goals. Your weekly goals break down your monthly goal into smaller do-able chunks. Your monthly goals help you reach your 90 day goals. Now use the 90 day stepping stones to help you reach your medium term goals.

What you want to do is reach your goals. This is important if you want financial freedom. You can modify change and drop your goals as you move forward.

See your goals as links in a chain; it is strongest when all of the links are joined.

My long-term goal is:

```

```

For this goal choose something that you can do in the next 6 months to 3 years.

My Goal for the medium term is:

```

```

What are your emotional reasons for reaching this goal?

You are motivated by the thrill of winning or by the fear of losing. What works best for you? Your emotion and its intensity can vary from goal to goal.

I want to achieve this goal because:

8

Long-term Goals

Linking goals helps you create better focus, and as a result, you will accomplish more in less time. Use this simple system and you will be amazed at the results.

Your long-term goal is something that you **can do** in the next 3 to 5 years..

You have your weekly goals or steps to help you achieve your goal. You use your monthly goals to help you take small steps towards making this dream become your reality. Long-term is anywhere from 6 months to five years.

Think of your goals as links, a chain is strongest when all of the links are joined. All of your goals strengthen when they move you closer to a long- term goal.

My long-term goal is:

>

Example:
My long-term goal is:

> Be Mortgage Free. My specific long term goal is to reduce my variable mortgage from 30 years to 20 years in the next four years.

You are an emotional person who uses logic as a tool to make things happen. It is your spiritual values that give true meaning to your life.

For this long-term goal, choose something that you can do in six months or longer.

My date for reaching my long-term goal is:

>

My date for reaching my long-term goal is:

> April 7th 2011.

What are your emotional reasons for reaching this goal?

You are motivated by the thrill of winning or by the fear of losing. The emotion and its intensity can vary from goal to goal. I am motivated by the thrill of winning. This is why I prefer to focus on the positives; many are motivated more by avoiding the negatives. What works best for you?

Your reasons can be factual, legal, emotional, spiritual or physical.

Include all of the positives or negatives for your goal. Why do you want to do this? You can be factual, legal, emotional, or spiritual. I prefer to focus on the positives; many are motivated more by avoiding the negatives. What works best for you?

I want to achieve this goal because:

I want to achieve this goal because:

- I want the freedom of choosing to work.
- I want the freedom of choosing what type of work I do and also where I work.
- I want the freedom of working in another country.
- I want to be free from the burden of making payments.
- I want to redirect my mortgage money into investments for my pension.
- With the variable part of our mortgage reduced we can do more work on our fixed half of our mortgage (which we have already reduced by ten years!).

LONG TERM GOALS

Linking your goals creates better focus, and you achieve more in less time.

Your long term goal is something that you **can do** in the next three to five years.

You will use your goal chain to accomplish this. You are using daily goals to help you reach your weekly goals. Your weekly goals break down your monthly goal into smaller do-able chunks. Your monthly goals help you reach your 90 day goals. Now use the 90 day stepping stones to help you reach your medium term goals.

What happens is you are constantly reviewing your goals and this makes it easier to reach your goals. Your daily do-able will move you closer to your long term goal.

What you want to do is reach your goals. This is important if you want financial freedom. You can modify change and drop your goals as you move forward.

See your goals as links in a chain; it is strongest when all of the links are joined. All of your goals strengthen when they move you closer to a long- term goal.

For this goal choose something that you can do in the next 3 to 5 years.

My Goal for the long term is:

You are motivated by the thrill of winning or by the fear of losing. What are your emotional reasons for reaching this goal? Be specific.

I want to achieve this goal because:

| |
| |
| |
| |
| |

9

Discover Daily Fun

▌ What do you get from Your Daily Fun Worksheet?

When I was a student and an aspiring agnostic, my mentor was Father Pat a Jesuit.

It was always stimulating talking to Pat but what changed my life is this simple tool. Every day for 5 to 15 minutes Pat would do something enjoyable that would elevate his mood and cost nothing. I have used this technique since then.

Now what Pat told me was that as a young man his superior had taught him this technique. But Pat rebelled against this because he loved studying so much. "I would just throw my pencil up in the air and catch it". And as a young man he felt that he had taken a break.

Many years later he lived close to the canal in Dublin. Every day he would walk by the canal. There are many religious benefits of being by the water, for example "he leads me beside the still waters". Water is a symbol of life, of growth and serenity.

When living in NYC, I would go for a walk into Central Park. If I felt at one with God I knew that I was on the right path. You will never get this experience by spending money. You will never develop the strength of character that comes from honouring your life with this simple tool.

In the worst periods of mankind's history man has sought fun and pleasure. Look around you today and you will see that this is true. History books record this.

Recently a friend of mine had a short term contract in a foreign country. It took him a number of weeks to put his finger on what was different. There was something wrong, but he couldn't work it out. One day having a coffee in a cosmopolitan café he saw the difference. The people didn't smile.

So what I am asking you to do is one simple activity every day that makes you feel better. Keep it simple and make it free. When you are listening to the music of life, and the music is beautiful, you wonder when the music will end. **The music stops playing when you stop listening.**

10

WHY YOU USE THE DAILY GRATITUDE JOURNAL

Many years ago I met Red Johnny. At one time in his life he had been homeless but was prospering when I met him.

Red Johnny was another of these spiritual people that I have been blessed to meet. You have to be grateful he would tell me. Here's the way it works. "When God gives me ten pence and I manage it well he gives me a pound. When I show him I can manage the pound he gives me ten pounds".

As a young man I did not want to hear about ten pence and a pound and then ten pounds, I wanted to hear about the big bucks. I was going places! What I have learnt since then is that Red Johnny was right. You work with what you have, you manage it well and then you get more.

I was at a church in NYC telling an old man about Red Johnny and this man told me that he wrote a gratitude list every night. "What are you grateful for?" he asked.

A while back I was staying in the home of a mega wealthy friend, and this is what he told me. "Every time that I give money, it comes back to me tenfold". And from my own experience and from observing others this is the secret ingredient of happy prosperity give and you shall prosper.

I'm not selling a bill of goods namely give me money and the Lord will bless you.

I am simply sharing with you an ageless truth, as you give life gives back to you by a large multiple. Was my friend right in saying it came back tenfold? I don't know. In my own life I think it has come back by a hundred fold.

When you give you give from a sense that you have more than enough. That is a pretty good place to be in. You may be very wealthy and planning to donate money to build a hospital. Alternatively you are in a place where the best use of your talents is to give some of your time. Either way you can give and prosper.

Use the gratitude journal to reflect back on your day and say thanks. It's a simple tool to transform your life. I have used it for decades and like all those before me I say just give it a try.

11

Your Daily Fun and Gratitude Journal

▌ **Transform your life with daily fun.**

How to create a life filled with joy and serenity.

Your life is a daily event. It's precious and we are only guaranteed today. My mother who is getting old has the same answer every day when I call her.

"How are you Mum?"

"Alive" she laughs.

And it is true, my mother understands the gift of life, we have it for today.

For decades I have used these tools, I didn't create them but I was willing to listen when people that I admired said this will improve your life.

The quality of our lives is often driven by simple actions. Below are two simple tools that will enrich your life, try them and see for your self.

What can you do today that is both fun and free?

| |
| |
| |

Example:

I will go for a half hour walk tonight. The weather forecast is good. Walking makes me feel great and I can review all of the day's actions. We have so much going on, so many new projects that walking is a form of meditation.

Create Your Daily Gratitude Journal.

Put Gratitude in your life and you will see how to solve insurmountable problems. You will not only see how you are blessed when compared to others but you will see that you always have something to be grateful no matter how dark the night. I can still the loud voice in my head.

I am grateful for today because: *(Try to fill in as many things as you can).*

| |
| |
| |
| |
| |

Example:

- *I have a wonderful family.*

- *When I came home from meeting a client kids were outside laughing and playing with their friends.*
- *Two new mortgage clients called me today.*

- *Met Fran for a cup of coffee, it was great to catch up and see how well things are going for him.*

- *Drove through beautiful countryside, was amazed at the beauty and grateful that I could both see and acknowledge this.*

- *Hooked up with a new VA (virtual assistant) referred by Goran in Chicago! What a wonderful world that we live in, where we can be interconnected with great people from all over the globe. My dad who had friends all over the world would have loved this. We live in amazing times.*

- *Started reading great new book.*

- *Tomorrow will be great.*

YOUR DAILY FUN AND GRATITUDE JOURNAL

▌ Transform your life with daily fun.

How to create a life filled with joy and serenity.

Your life is a daily event. It's precious and we are only guaranteed today.

The quality of our lives is often driven by simple actions. Below are two simple tools that will enrich your life, try them and see for your self.

What can you do today that is both fun and free?

| |
| |
| |
| |
| |

Create Your Daily Gratitude Journal.

Put Gratitude in your life and you will see how to solve insurmountable problems. You will not only see how you are blessed when compared to others but you will see that you always have something to be grateful no matter how dark the night.

I am grateful for today because: *(Try to fill in as many things as you can).*

| |
| |
| |
| |
| |

12

WHEN DO YOU PUT A GOAL OR DREAM ON THE SHELF?

There are times when you have a great idea and it keeps you awake at night. And yet it is something that you can't do right now.

This is the place where you put those ideas down in writing. When the time is right you can take them down and start an action plan to make it happen.

This program is for your life. It's not just about money. Money affects every area of your life, and it is used in and created by the accomplishments of your goals.

What type of goals can you put on the shelf?

- *I want to take a year off work and write a novel.*
- *I want to travel across the world.*

- *I want to work for a charity in the developing world.*

- *We want to build an extension.*

- *We want the latest and greatest TV wonder screen.*

- *Going on a three day weekend to Paris.*

- *Buying new chairs for the kitchen.*

- *Going to the three day never to be repeated seminar.*

- *Starting a part time business.*

The list is endless, and it goes from the mundane to life changing. What they share in common is that you would like to do them today. This is a living list, items go on, and others are taken off (like going to Paris with your now ex).

Example:

- *New bookkeeping software for business owners. Too many irons in the fire. Can do this later. Need to remain focused.*

- *Marketing seminar in Atlanta. Love to go, but this is not the right time. Don't have the time, money invested better in current projects.*

- *Pension letter for clients. Again just don't have the time for the follow up work that will be required.*

PART 3

NEW MONEY SKILLS

How to get out of debt and prosper

Today we are swamped with debt, relationships end, families are broken and businesses are destroyed by debt repayments. Anyone can borrow it is repaying a loan that is hard.

Money is a mood changer. Once you accept this you understand why you borrow. Spending for most of us is fun. Buying today is better than buying tomorrow.

On top of this we have had an endless stream of "gurus" sell us nonsense like the concept of good debt and bad debt. We have been fed an endless stream of lies about how the market performs. And they say don't pay off your mortgage instead invest this money for a higher return in the market. This is total nonsense.

People have borrowed because they believed that the sun will always shine.

In the middle ages we had slavery by way of feudalism. The rich and the powerful were rich and powerful because this was God's will. The rest of us starved and worked for their pleasure.

Today lenders are the rich and powerful. And we have a new dogma, you can't argue with success. I believe that until you are free from the clutches of the money lenders and the "gurus" who do their bidding you will have to work.

I have nothing against borrowing. If you want to borrow go ahead. I have borrowed and will borrow but with great care. If you want to be debt free this book is for you. Use this section and I will blow you away. Many of you will end your mortgage by three or four years using just an extra fiver a week.

When your mortgage is gone use this money to prepare for an early retirement.

Everything that you need to create a spending plan; or how to save or build wealth to retirement savings tools are in here. You can change your life with these tools. Your true income work-

sheet should amaze you.

I

FIND YOUR TRUE HOURLY INCOME

Knowing your true hourly income will affect every major money decision. From where you live to where you work, this is affected by your true hourly income.

I have met many clients who told me that the cheaper home cost them more, more time in travelling, extra costs for travelling to work, higher car maintenance costs from the wear and tear of the additional miles, and of course higher costs for fuel.

You already understand this principle; and we're expanding this to all costs for working. Every step you take with your money is determined by your income and then by your spending. There are many hidden expenses with how you make your money. Our goal is to discover those. You will then discover your real net income.

Start by reading the questions below.

Then look at the example that I have done for you. You can use this to help you fill in your own answers. A word of warning; be prepared to be surprised!

I am giving you a low cost tool to help you create major improvements in your life. And these improvements are easy to implement. You will look at your work with new eyes after this. It's a hands on exercise and you will feel the results instantly.

Enough talking, it's time for action. Are you ready? Good. This will be interesting.

Step One

We want to find out how much time you spend in total on work activities.

How many hours do you spend each week on work?	
How many hours do you spend travelling to your work?	
How many hours do you work each week?	
Add these two to get your total.	
This is the amount of time that you spend earning your income.	

Step Two

What is your current income?
We want to find out how much you actually make. We are using weekly numbers. If you are paid monthly, multiply your monthly income by twelve and then divide by 52 to get your weekly income.

What is your gross weekly income before taxes?	
What is your weekly income after taxes?	

Step Three

How much does it cost you to work?
To help us find your true weekly income we want to deduct your expenses that are directly related to your work. If you quit working you wouldn't have these expenses

What are your costs to get to work?	

These expenses can be rail, bus or the cost of petrol.

If you use a car what are your costs of car maintenance?	

(Take your annual costs of car maintenance and divide by 52. If your car is used for both work and personal use, use a pro rata figure. So if you use your car like I do for 80% work you multiply your costs by .80).

How much do you spend on work lunches?	
How much do you spend on work treats to release stress?	

(Treats like cappuccinos, muffins, magazines, books. You spend this money because you are working so hard and you feel that you need a treat to compensate).

What is your weekly spend on educational items related to your work?	

(These are items like professional magazines, seminars, courses. You wouldn't have these expenses if you weren't working. This helps in planning for your retirement).

How much do you spend on work clothes?	

Do you wear these clothes on the weekend?)

If you use child care, how much does this cost you?	
List and total any other work related expenses here.	
Now add these expenses to get your total	

Step Four
Discover Your True Income

We deduct your weekly work expenses from the total in step three	
We go back to step one and put your net weekly income here	
This gives us your true net weekly income	
We go to step one and put the number of hours spent working here	
Now we divide your income by the number of hours spent on work here	
This gives us your true hourly income.	

How do you feel about this number?
Are you surprised at your hourly income? Did you think it was higher?

Step Five

You want to discover the monthly time cost for your loan payments.

How much do you spend each month on your loan repayments?	

If you are married or cohabiting enter your share of the loan payments.

What is your true hourly income?	
Divide your loan repayments by your true hourly income.	

This tells us how many hours you must spend working each month just to make your loan repayments. Many of you will be shocked at this number.

- How do you feel about this number?
- Does this motivate you to become debt free?

For many of you seeing this number if you are not immediately shocked into having a burning desire to become debt free I don't know what will motivate you to living a debt free life.

Here is the key question from this worksheet.

- *Are You a Debt Slave today?*
  (The emphasis is on today).

Our goal is to change your reality. I have done this, you can do it.

Here is what you can take away that is a life changing positive.

If you can see how little that you are actually making, then you can see how easy it is to become financially independent. Use this program to get rid of your loan payments, reduce or eliminate your work related expenses, and you have the freedom to choose. You can choose whether to work, and what you want to work at. For most people this is just a pipedream, for you it can be reality.

Later I will show you what you need to save to become financially independent. We have separate worksheets for this.

We have an example done for you, so just follow along and do it for yourself. It is not important that you get it perfect, you can finesse the details later. If you have to start with estimates do so. A bad start is far better and more useful than a perfect procrastination. Start now, do it perfectly later, if you are a perfectionist.

2

FIND YOUR TRUE HOURLY INCOME; AN EXAMPLE

Knowing your true hourly income will affect every major money decision. From where you live to where you work, this is affected by your true hourly income.

Imagine this scenario. You make €1,000 per week for 40 hours of work. I ask you how much you make and you say you make €25 per hour because €25 per hour for forty hours is €1,000.

"Wait a minute" I say, "how much time do you spend travelling to work"?

You tell me ten hours so really you spend 50 hours in total on work. This means that you now make €20 per hour because €1,000 divided by 50 hours is €20.

I get it you say. I really only make €20 per hour.

This is a great step in seeing what your true hourly income is. Now let's see what really happens. This step is easy to do and it's a practical step in creating healthy money.

Start by reading the questions below.

Then look at the example that I have done for you. You can use this to help you fill in your own answers. A word of warning; be prepared to be surprised!

I am giving you a low cost tool to help you create major improvements in your life. And these improvements are easy to implement. You will look at your work with new eyes after this. It's a hands on exercise and you will feel the results instantly.

Enough talking, it's time for action. Are you ready? Good.

This will be interesting.

Step One
How many hours do you spend each week on work?
We want to find out how much time you spend in total on work activities.

How many hours do you spend travelling to your work?	10
How many hours do you work each week?	40

Add these two to get your total.	50

This is the amount of time that you spend earning your income.
Step Two

What is your current income?
We want to find out how much you actually make. We are using weekly numbers. If you are paid monthly, multiply your monthly income by twelve and then divide by 52 to get your weekly income

What is your gross weekly income before taxes?	€1000
What is your weekly income after taxes?	€800

Step Three

How much does it cost you to work?
To help us find your true weekly income we want to deduct your expenses that are directly related to your work. If you quit working you wouldn't have these expenses.

What are your costs to get to work?	€50

These expenses can be rail, bus or the cost of petrol.

If you use a car what are your costs of car maintenance?	€21

(Take your annual costs of car maintenance and divide by 52. If your car is used for both work and personal use, use a pro rata figure.

So if you use your car like I do for 80% work you multiply your costs by .80).

How much do you spend on work lunches?	€27
How much do you spend on work treats to release stress?	€12

(Treats like cappuccinos, muffins, magazines, books. You spend this money because you are working so hard and you feel that you need a treat to compensate).

How much do you spend on work clothes?	€10

(Do you wear these clothes on the weekend?)

If you use child care, how much does this cost you?	€0
List and total any other work related expenses here.	€3
Now add these expenses to get your total.	€151

Step Four

Discover Your True Income

We go back to step one and put your net weekly income here	€800
We deduct your weekly work expenses from the total in step three	€138

This gives us you true net weekly income	€662
We go to step one and put the number of hours spent working here	€50
Now we divide your income €662 by the number of hours 70 spent on work	€13.24

This gives us your true hourly income €13.24

- How do you feel about this number?
- Are you surprised at your hourly income? Did you think it was higher?

Step Five

You want to discover the monthly time cost for your loan payments.

How much do you spend each month on your loan repayments?	€358

If you are married or cohabiting enter your share of the loan payments.

What is your true hourly income?	€10.42
Divide your loan repayments €358 by your true hourly income €13.24 =	27.04

This tells us how many hours you must spend working each month just to make your loan repayments. Many of you will be shocked at this number.

In this example you work 27 hours each month just to make loan payments

- How do you feel about this number?
- Does this motivate you to become debt free?

For many of you seeing this number if you are not immediately shocked into having a burning desire to become debt free I don't know what will motivate you to living a debt free life.

Before you did this exercise if I asked you how much you earned per hour you would have said €25 per hour. (40 hours x €25 = €1,000)

If I said include your travel time of ten hours your pay went down to €20 per hour. You were still feeling good about your income.

Sadly you now see that your true hourly income is only €13.24 And you now see that you spend 27 hours a month paying your personal loans. This doesn't include your mortgage payment! Remember your personal loan only costs you €358 per month. This changes your perspective on loan payments. For example is that new car worth 27 hours of work each and every month. With healthy money only you can decide, but now you have the tools for a better decision.

Here is the key question from this worksheet.

- *Are You a Debt Slave today?*
  (The emphasis is on today).

Our goal is to change your reality. I have done this, you can do it.

Here is what you can take away that is a life changing positive.

If you can see how little that you are actually making, then you

can see how easy it is to become financially independent. Use

this program to get rid of your loan payments, reduce or elimi-

nate your work related expenses, and you have the freedom to

choose. You can choose whether to work, and what you want to

work at. For most people this is just a pipedream, for you it can

be reality.

Later I will show you what you need to save to become finan-

cially independent. We have separate worksheets for this.

We have an example done for you, so just follow along and do it

for yourself. It is not important that you get it perfect, you can

finesse the details later. If you have to start with estimates do so.

A bad start is far better and more useful than a perfect procrasti-

nation. Start now, do it perfectly later, if you are a perfectionist.

3

INVESTIGATE YOUR FIXED MONTHLY EXPENSES

▌ Take a new look.

Before, we start, there's one question that must be answered.

Would you work for someone who? _____ _____ _____

Read the question below and fill in the blanks above.

Would you work for someone who <u>NEVER</u> <u>PAID</u> <u>YOU?</u>

No, you would not. You can go to jail for not paying employees their just wages.

You pay the phone bill, the electricity bill, the tax man, the grocery store each and every month. We pay our loans but many of us refuse to pay ourselves. Here's the rub, if you never save you never pay yourself. You pay yourself when you save.

From today your goal is to pay yourself each and every time that you get paid. One goal is to save 10 per cent of your income. Our goal today is to start. You can pick an amount, like €100 or a percentage like 5%. Just pick and stick to it like glue.

It is one thing to say "pay yourself first" and it is another to do so. The last line is to be filled in with the amount that you are going to pay yourself. Today this may be a very small amount, and that's okay. As you improve, you'll give yourself a pay raise. I'm just curious: When you fill in the blanks below do the numbers increase?

If you said no and you've been working, don't worry, we will create a new you because you'll take new actions. They will give you better results and they will impact and improve every area of your life from the workplace to your bedroom.

Your savings record

Ten years ago I saved		per month.
Five years ago I saved		per month.
One year ago I saved		per month.

Today I will save		per month.

Enter a figure that you can commit to on the line above.

Our goal with the fixed monthly expenses worksheet is to find what you are absolutely committed to spending every month.

These are the things that you have no choice over. Later you may decide to cancel some items and increase your spending on others such as savings or your prepayment of taxes if you are always short at tax time. Alternatively you may decide to get your taxes reduced by opening a retirement account.

Your goal is simple; just fill in all of your fixed monthly expenses. There are many blanks so that this can be tailored exactly to fit your lifestyle.

A fixed expense is one that is the same every month and you have to pay it every month. You may have child care expenses or you may belong to a club that has monthly dues.

You may not remember every expense the first time and that's okay. We are moving in the right direction.

Fill in all of the items NOW.

When you spend your money the key question is always;

Are you receiving emotional value for your money?

When you are in doubt about buying an impulse item, the second question is;

What is my true hourly income?

When you translate the cost into hours and minutes of work, this helps you decide if this is a good buy for you.

If it is; go for it, enjoy.

This is a joy based program.

Your fixed monthly expenses worksheet.
In the first item put pay myself.

Fixed Expenses	Amount
1. From today I will pay myself	
2. Home (mortgage or rent)	
3. Health insurance	
4. Life insurance	

5.	Car insurance	
6.	TV (cable or satellite)	
7.	Gym	
8.	Education	
9.	Bank charges	
10.	Taxes	
11.	Pension	
12.	Club memberships	
13.	Magazine subscriptions	
14.	Other subscriptions	
15.	Other	
16.	Other	
17.	Other	
18.	Other	
19.	Other	

You can download more copies at www.advisordomain.com/book

4

WHAT ARE YOUR MONTHLY LOAN PAYMENTS?

Our first step towards becoming debt free is to record all loans and debts.

Extra amount that you cay pay	
Car loan	
Personal loan	
Credit card 1	
Credit card 2	
home improvement loan	
Holiday loan	
Credit Union	
Other	
Other	

As you can see the very first item is for the extra amount that you can pay each month. Your goal is to find a minimum amount to reduce your debt.

You can put coins in a jar and use those coins each week or each month to reduce your loans. You may change your spending habits to get maximum enjoyment for your money. My goal is to help you create a joy filled life. Getting out of debt is a huge step, and for most people who do not read this book it will only be a pipe dream, a mere late night fantasy. Stay with me because you will become debt free.

This is the same principle as paying yourself first. It is easier said than done. I want you to make a commitment as solid as your other loan payments.

If you have a variable loan where the payments can rise and fall depending on your interest rate you would not call your lender to say sorry I can't find an extra €5 per week. Most of you can find that extra €5 per week.

5

WHAT ARE YOUR VARIABLE MONEY EXPENSES?

Our goal here is to look at how you spend. You may need to track your spending.

- My goal is to get you to understand that when you are overspending in one area you are under spending in another area of your life.

For example, if you're a smoker you may spend less on new clothes or home decoration than a non smoker. One of the great myths perpetuated by financial gurus is that if you just stop smoking you can fund a pension. What happens is that you re-direct your spending. Such as; you furnish your home, or you eat out more.

The key to improving your spending is to ask am I getting emotional value for my money. We go into this in the joy filled spending plan.

Variable expenses recorder

Clothing	
Food from stores	
Food out	
Books	
Entertainment	
Music	
Lotions and potions	
Hair	
Bathroom necessities	
Household goods	
Other	
Other	

Creating a healthy money Y.O.U spending plan.

A step by step example

Category	Forecast	Actual	EV
Income Insurance	194	194	Yes
Health Insurance	160	160	Yes
Car Insurance	120	120	Yes
Life Insurance	138	138	Yes
Taxes	850	600	Under
Pension	250	0	Under
Heat	65	85	Over
Electricity	86	97	Over
Household Goods	28	37	Over
Home Maintenance	75	0	Under
Transport	310	335	Over
Newspapers	28	56	Over
Entertainment	85	0	Over

Eating Out	160	223	Over
Coffee Out	29	75	Over
Books	35	67	Over
Basic Groceries	650	694	Yes
Meat	39	37	Under
Children's Schooling	48	54	Yes
Children's Gifts	45	76	Over
Children's Clothes	84	84	Yes
Adult Clothes	96	41	Under
Dental	70	70	Yes
Mortgage	1108	1108	Yes
Hair	160	120	Under
Gift Account	65	40	Under

Now fill in your spending plan.

It's a work in progress.

You'll overspend and under spend. Before you start look at how I recorded emotional value for my money.

What do the signs Y O and U mean? I just use the first initial for my records.

Y or Yes Means that my spending in this area is just right.

O or Over Means that I would get more enjoyment by spending less here.

U or Under This means I am not spending enough on this category. I am under spending, and my enjoyment will increase if I spend more on this area.

What happened this month? Clearly I was overspending in areas equivalent to comfort food.

Areas that I overspent:

This is Comfort Spending.

- Heat. Oil costs more. Maybe it's time to get better insulation.

- Newspapers. Bought lots to make me feel informed and relieve work stress.

- Magazines, exact same reason.

- Coffee out. Same reason, working so hard I needed regular caffeine pickups, with muffins or donuts.

- Eating out. A sure sign that my life is out of whack. You may have different areas for comfort spending.

- Children's gifts. Was it more parties than usual or am I just dreaming about the cost of gifts? Do I need to increase the amount for this category?

- Groceries. Prices are up, but I'm happy that I stuck to my lists. Normally under pressure at work I load up on junk food treats.

Where did I under spend?

This is where you deprive yourself of things that would improve your life.

If you overspend in one area you will subconsciously under spend in another area, in a desperate move to stay on budget. This means that you overspend in areas of low emotional feedback but the feedback or emotional high is immediate. And you under spend on those things that help your self esteem.

Areas that I under spent:

- Taxes. Not smart. The tax man does not go away.

- Clothes. An easy one to dispense with. If your clothes don't make you feel great, they will eventually make you feel less than. This is where emotional value is really useful.

- Entertainment. I would have preferred to go the movies with my wife; instead I blew the entertainment money on books, coffee and newspapers.

- Pension. Rationalized that I'd catch up next month. Have you done this?

- Home Maintenance. It's easier to save money monthly versus the big bill.

- Hair. For women this can be a very big emotional issue. It's important for us men but nowhere as impactful on our self esteem.

So you get the idea. This is to improve your life; it's not a stick to beat you with.

I only track my daily spending if I need a financial tune up. If I stick to the basics such as shopping with a list, and I shop after I've eaten things go well. I am not a tracker but I will do it on occasion. If I'm saving and paying my taxes, mortgage, and bills then I feel that I have the right to blow my money any way I want.

When I say I, this means we because my family is the real part of this equation.

The number one tool to stop you blowing money on impulse is to know your true hourly income. If it's ten Euro an hour then you blow 30 minutes of work on a magazine that costs you five Euro. This simple tool will improve how you spend.

The second tool is to ask "am I getting emotional value for this buy"? Yes? Go for it.

You can use this spending plan for your work if you are self employed.

I only track the big items, but I use the emotional value on all impulse buys. I do this because this is where I have had the most problems.

This is your healthy money spending plan.

Copy or download this as often as you like.

Category	Forecast	Actual	EV

6

How to create a joy based Y.O.U. spending plan

Spending money is fun. Once we accept this we can change our spending choices. The key to having more fun is simply to make different choices.

We all know the stereotype of comfort food; your partner dumps you and out comes the tub of ice cream. Look at your friends who have broken up after a long term relationship and look at their actions. We would never criticize them; we would accept that this is a phase that they are going through.

I believe that we take the same type of actions with our spending when we're under stress.

Just as you put away the tub of ice cream when a new person comes into your life your old spending patterns will disappear when a better way of managing money comes into your life.

An error is an error and when it is pointed out it disappears back into nothingness. When we learn as children that two and two is four; we never go back to thinking that the answer might be three or even five.

When we learn that the world is round we can never accept that the world is flat. I can remember our teachers explaining that the sailors thought that if they sailed out too far they would fall off the edge of the world. Now we lived by the ocean and the sea was always a place of mystery and adventure. When you looked out as far as you could see the ocean did seem to fall over. So it was easy to imagine a sailor having this fear.

I want you to understand that you can become a person who puts money to work. If you don't put money to work, sadly you will always work for money.

The only time that I believe in tracking your money is when you don't know where it's going. Now I'm sure that if you tracked every penny and then fastidiously put every penny to work in its correct category you'd have more but I don't do this.

The key to tracking is to ask one question and one question only;

Are you getting emotional value for your money?

Now there are only three answers:
1. Y. I'm getting just the right amount.
2. O. I'm overspending. I should spend less on this category; I'm not getting that much joy from it.
3. U. I should spend more on this category; I get a lot of joy from this.

I think of this as being a Y, O or U.

There is one vital part of this equation:

What is your true net pay per hour? You got this answer from your true income worksheet. You want to know how much work time you'll spend on an impulse buy.

Typically we get into trouble with impulse buys, but you can use this anywhere. So if I spend eighty work hours a month on my home; am I getting Emotional Value?

This principle of EV allows you to choose exactly how you spend your money. Occasionally put this into your daily do-able worksheet. This is not a stick to beat yourself with; it is a healthy money tool to help you get more joy from your spending.

As you go through life your spending patterns change.

When you graduate from college you need a place to live, and this is a huge amount of your money.

You buy your first home and you have a whole new range of spending choices, from furniture to maintenance. Every time you spend money in these areas you have less to blow on weekends away which you did before you bought your home.

You have children and a new world of spending opens up from food to education.

You get older and your retirement is a big factor in how you spend your money.

This is why I have no guidelines on how you should spend your money. I want you to use the goal system to help you create a better life. You'll have more awareness of what you're doing. Your age and circumstances determine how you spend.

If you are attracted to the big city lights and you take a low paying job to pursue your passion then housing will eat up a huge portion of your income. The person making this choice gets tremendous emotional and spiritual satisfaction from pursuing their dreams. Another young person lives and works in a small town, gets on the housing ladder many years earlier and is also enriched.

Your job is to decide if this is right or wrong. No one else can do this for you.

Every time that you spend on one area of your life this prevents you from spending on another. So the question that creates equality is "are you getting emotional value for your money?"

To answer this question you must know your true hourly income.

For example let's assume that you are making €10 per hour and your impulse buy costs you €5. This means that you must work for 30 minutes to buy this item.

In our example your true hourly income was only €13.24 per hour. So if this €13.24 number is in your head, you will think twice before you blow €5 on a coffee and a muffin. This treat will cost you 20 minutes of your life.

Is it worth it? Only you can say yes or no.

That €5 purchase is probably a no brainer if you make €100 per hour. As you honour the time it took to make money, you'll say no, I will not blow my money.

In Summary:

- What is your true net pay per hour?

- How much of your working life will this cost you?

- Are you getting emotional value for your money?

- This is a no shame, no blame program. We are all different. Your needs, wants and desires change as you go through the game of life.

- Track your spending if you want to see where your money is going. You've worked hard for it so this is the least that you should know. Once you begin to save systematically and continuously you are freed from needing to know where every penny went.

Good luck and please let me know has this helped you

7

What steps do you take now to create a Y.O.U. spending plan?

You need to know where you are before so that you have a clear picture of what you can do. You simply fill out the following worksheets;

- Monthly loan payments
- Fixed monthly expenses
- Variable monthly expenses.

Our goal is to not only to remove monthly loan payments from your life but to keep them out of your life. You may have no control over your fixed monthly expenses but your housing costs can vary. What if you took in a roommate?

Variable expenses show you where you have the most control over your spending.

Our goal when rebuilding or in reality rebranding your life is to filter our choices through the emotional value tool. Am I getting emotional value for my money?

This is why I think that hiring people above the level you need is a waste of your hard earned money. Hiring a world class lawyer to do a routine will is a waste of money.

You have hired an expert to do journey man work.

You are rebranding you because you are in the process of becoming a person who makes money work for you instead of you working for money. Inside your head you will not argue with the notion that you are in the process of becoming because this allows you to take baby steps. As you improve you'll take bigger steps.

DEBT BE GONE MIND MAP

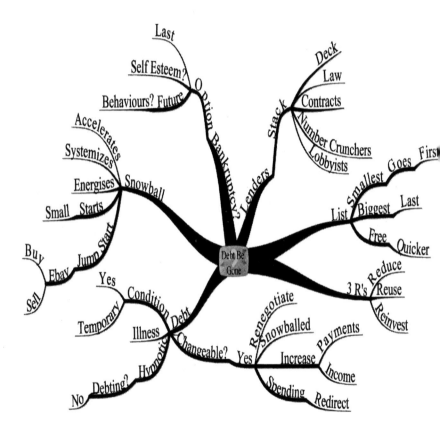

This mind map shows the way out of debt and all of the benefits you get from taking small consistent actions

9

HOW TO GET OUT OF DEBT AND LIVE FREE

▌ Borrowing money is easy, paying it back is hard.

Modern society is fuelled by debt; we are fed nonsense such as good debt and bad debt. This plays to our desire to be good boys and good girls. We are responsible adults, inside our head our little voice says "you can count on me". This attitude normally helps us but now it leads us slowly but surely into debt slavery.

The deck is stacked against us. We compete against big banks who hire the best and the brightest number wizards. They make sure that the bank always wins.

The basic loan agreement is a contract written by the lender to protect the lender. They can dream up any type of extra charge from an early payment fee to a late payment fee. You need to know that the deck is stacked against you.

Your job is to break free from their clutches. So it's time to begin.

Part A

What you need to do to become debt free

Step One Make a list.

You make a list of every loan and debt with your balance and monthly payment.

Later you get a worksheet to complete but for now a blank piece of paper works.

If you can, put in the interest rate on each loan.

Step Two Write these loans in order from smallest to largest.

The loan that you owe the smallest amount on goes in as number one. You continue until you have your largest loan as last.

Step Three Find your extra payment

This is where your commitment to being debt free becomes tangible. How much extra can you afford to pay each month on your loans? The greater your desire to be debt free the greater this sum of money should be.

You may be swamped with loan repayments and feel that there is no hope. If you are swamped today you will be swamped tomorrow. Something must change or else you face many years of being crushed by your debt repayments.

Pick a number, any number no matter how small and stick to it. Remember the law of the irreducible minimum? This states that if you want to change the amount of time that you will be a in debt you must make an extra payment.

So how do you find an extra payment?

- Save loose coins in a jar.
- Work overtime.
- Redirect your spending. Make every penny work for you. Use the emotional value tool to help you get more enjoyment from your spending. If you spend thirty Euro a month on magazines and you have no money to pay extra should you reconsider? Are the magazines worth a lifetime of debt?
- Only shop with a shopping list. Only buy what is on the list.
- Do your shopping on the days when prices are lowest. My local supermarket has discounts on a Wednesday.
- Physically shop less often. The less you shop the less you spend. Try it.
- Find out what your impulse buys are. Drill into your head what your emotional value is for these items.
- Understand your true hourly income. Use this tool to spend less on impulse.

- Get another job. Don't do this forever. You want to have a family life; a work slave is not much different than a debt slave.
- Create a new income from a part time business. What do you know that someone else would like to learn? From recipes to how to do your job or business better, you have something that people will buy.
- Sell on eBay your old clothes or unwanted collectibles, furniture or antiques.
- Create crafts to sell part time.
- Teach an evening course. What do you know that we would like to learn?
- Set up a babysitting service for teenagers to do the work. You verify the teenagers for the parents who want a baby sitter.
- Be creative. See what other people are doing at www.advisordomain.com/forum

Step Four Use the Snowball effect

A rolling stone gathers no moss. It is easier to roll down a hill than to climb a hill. We are going to use this principle to help you become debt free.

One of the myths about getting out of debt is that you start with your highest interest loan and work from there. Our software on our site debunks this myth. Mathematically it pretty much makes no difference which way you go about it.

Using human math there is an enormous difference.

We all like to win, and this is a program designed to create winners. It is easier to stick with a program when you are constantly removing debts from your life. In real life if you start with your highest interest loan you may never get out of debt. You will never see tangible progress from that extra fifty that you send every month. With no visible progress you will quit.

This means that as one loan is paid your payment from the first loan is added to the second. When the second loan is completed this payment is added to the third.

Here is a simple example.

Loans	Balance	Monthly Payment	Extra Payment	Total Payment
Car Loan	€1,500	€250	€50	€300

When the car loan is finished the entire car payment of €300 is added to the furniture loan.

Furniture	€1,600	€190	€300	€490

When the furniture loan is finished the entire furniture payment of €490 is added to the credit card payment. This rises from an eternal payment of €75 to €565 which will get you out of credit card hell.

Credit card	€6,000	€75	€490	€565

Later in the worksheets we will show you how to work out exactly how quickly you will go from debt slave to being a debt free human being.

Use this debt freedom worksheet to get started

We have numbered each column in bold to make it easier to follow. This is easy to do.

Loan / Debt	Amount (1)	Monthly payment (2)	Extra PM (3)	Total PM (4) = (2)+(3)
Debt X	50,000	490	100	590
Mortgage				
Car Payment				
Credit card				

copyright Gerard Malone 2008

As you can see above we have a loan called debt x, we have a balance of 50,000, our monthly payment is 490, and we can pay an extra 100 per month. This means that we can pay 590 per month and this is recorded in our last column, column 4.

For now enter your loans in any order.

Below you can put them in order from the lowest amount owed to the largest.
After this in Debt Worksheet B we will show you how long it takes to become debt free.
Now write your loans and debts in order from the smallest to the largest.
We will now use the debt freedom worksheet.

Your debt freedom worksheet

Loan / Debt	Amount (1)	Monthly payment (2)	Extra PM (3)	Total PM (4) = (2)+(3)	Annual Payments (5) = (4) x (12)
Debt X	50,000	490	100	590	7080
Smallest					
Largest					

If you look above you will see that we have added one small step.
In the last column we want to know what your annual payment on this loan is. Simply multiply your monthly payment by 12. Debt X has a monthly payment of 590. When we multiply 590 by 12 we get 7,080.

Later we will use this to find out how long it will take you to get out of debt.

How long will it take you to get out of debt?

We are now going to use Debt Freedom Worksheet B.

What we are going to do is very simple. We are going to divide the balance owed by your annual payment.

In Debt X we owe 50,000 and we divide this by our annual payment of 7,080. This gives us 7.06. Then we look at our debt freedom table to see how long it will take us to repay this loan.

Debt Freedom Worksheet B

Annual Payments (5) = (4)x(12)	Amount Payments (6) = (1)/(5)	Interest Rate (7)	Years Remaining (from tables below)
7080	7.06	10%	12 years

Steps Needed:

- Fill in your loans one at a time
- Fill in the interest rate. It is okay to make a mistake on this, you can correct this later. For now we want to keep moving forward.
- We look at the table below to see how long it takes us to become debt free.

Interest Rate	Years to pay						
	1	5	10	15	20	25	30
5%	0.95	4.33	7.72	10.38	12.46	14.09	15.37
10%	0.91	3.79	**6.14**	**7.61**	8.51	9.08	9.43
15%	0.87	3.35	5.02	5.85	6.26	6.46	6.57
20%	0.83	2.99	4.19	4.68	4.87	4.95	4.98

To determine your years remaining, find the row nearest to your interest rate. Then, find the value nearest (6), and the column gives you the years remaining.

We will go back to debt x:

We divided 50,000 by 7,080 and we got 7.16. We recorded this in column 6.

Our interest rate is 10%. When we look at the table above we can see that 7.06 is between 10 and 15 years. You see them above in bold. We'll guess that it is 12 years.For an exact figure use our software on www.advisordomain.com/book

Again we are using the law of the irreducible minimum, we want to move forward and become debt free. For today we do not need to be exact we just want to see where we stand. This tool allows you to do this with a pencil and calculator.

Do this one step at a time, one loan at a time. See how quickly you get this done.

On our website we have free worksheets for you. Please bear with me if you hate numbers this is very simple. This is the key to your financial freedom.

Fast Track Debt Free 12 week coaching program

This is a 12 week group coaching program done over the phone and internet. You will use the full goal setting tools, and fast track debt reduction techniques in a friendly setting.

You'll move from being in debt to becoming debt free. You determine how fast you'll move and how many new actions you'll take.

By focusing on what can be done and actually getting this done you change your life. Maybe you want to fast track debt freedom or possibly you're overwhelmed with debts. My philosophy based on my own life story is that you are not a debtor but a person with debts. This is a situation or life condition you can change today.

It is the journey that enriches you. Once you understand that you will become financially free all is changed. You'll live in a whole new world, no longer whipped around like a leaf in a storm. You make your own choices no longer swayed by the pied pipers of guruism offering quick and easy wealth.

At the end of 12 weeks you will have changed your internal compass, you will be grounded as a saver. You will be used to taking daily actions that move you towards a specific weekly goal. The weekly goals will help you achieve your monthly goal. And three months later you will achieve your quarterly goal.

Do you want a fast kick start to being debt free? This coaching is for people like you. 12 weeks can change your life and put you on the path to creating a life that you only dream of. Your dreams are something you can choose to achieve.

If you are ready to become debt free email to

debtfree@advisordomain.com

IO

FOR PROSPERITY OPEN YOUR SAVINGS TOOLBOX

Here lies the key to achieving your investment goals. It doesn't matter whether you are saving for your child's education or for a new car; this is the tool that works.

If the savings toolbox is the engine to help you achieve your dreams, then the goal worksheets are the fuel.

Self honesty is the glue that binds together your goals and savings. If you are saying that your goal is to save €25,000 over the next five years and you buy on impulse the latest apple gizmo then you are in conflict. Your spending choices are not only in competition but you are in conflict with your desire to save.

Supposing you want to buy some new, must have high priced item. You set this as a short term goal. Are you in conflict with your long term goal of saving €25,000 in five years? Not necessarily you may choose to cut back on other variable spending choices. Maybe you don't buy that suit or you postpone home repairs.

Healthy money is about making choices and understanding that you can't have it all now.

How do you use the savings toolbox?

You have two saving choices. You can either save a fixed amount each month for any period you like or you find out how much you need to save to reach your goal.

In example one; you want to have €25,000 saved in five years and you think that you will make 10% a year on your money. By using the saving worksheet you see that you need to save €322.83 per month. We'll do examples in the next chapter.

If the growth on your money was only 7.5% you need to save €344.68 each month.

In example two; you want to save €300 per month for five years and you think you should make 10% a year on your money. The worksheet says you'll have €23,232

You can clearly see that you can work out any savings goal that you want to accomplish.

Our goal is to give you the tools you need to create a life of financial freedom. And financial freedom is always defined in your terms and driven by your values.

11

How to use your savings toolbox

▌ A step by step guide with examples

Our goal is to show you two ways to create prosperity. First we show you how much you need to save to reach a specific lump sum. The second is to see how much you'll get if you save the same amount each month.

To do this we use the table below. You can do this with a pencil and calculator.

Interest Rate	Years invested						
	1	5	10	15	20	30	40
2.5 %	12.14	63.84	136.17	218.12	310.97	535.37	823.46
5.0 %	12.28	**68.01**	155.28	267.29	411.03	832.26	1526.02
7.5 %	12.42	72.53	177.93	331.11	553.73	1347.45	3023.82
10.0 %	12.57	77.44	204.84	414.47	759.37	2260.49	6324.08

194

You have two factors. On top we've the number of years that you'll save for. On the left side we've four different interest rates or rates of growth if you're investing.

You have a specific goal; **you want to buy a car for cash in 5 years.**

Let's get started. Here are the five steps we take

You want to save for a specific goal	
1. What is the amount that you want to have?	€25,000
2. What is the interest rate that you will get for your money?	5%
3. How many years do you have to save for this goal?	Five years
4. Look at the table at 5 percent and where it meets 5 years.	68.01
5. To find out how much you need to save you: **Divide your desired amount €25,000 by 68.01**	= 367.59

You need to save €368 per month for five years to reach your goal of €25,000

Here is a quick recap:
- You want to have €25,000
- You will earn 5% on your savings.
- You have five years to save.
- The value on the table is 68.01
- You divided your desired €25,000 by 68.01 and you got 367.59

This means you save €368 a month for 5 years to reach your goal of €25,000.

This is where honesty steps in. Do you really want to save €25,000 in five years? Is this a realistic goal? Only you can decide. If €368 per month was too much you can change the time or you redirect your spending so you can save €368 per month.

Five years is a short investment time period. So if you chase a high rate of return you may lose everything. You have little time to recover a drop in its value.

Now it's your turn:

You want to save for a specific goal	
1. What is the amount that you want to have?	
2. What is the interest rate that you will get for your money?	%
3. How many years do you have to save for this goal?	__ years
4. Look at the table at percent and where it meets __years. *(First fill in the per cent value and the number of years).*	
5. To find out how much you need to save you: **Divide your desired amount ------by interest rate on table**	

I need to save   per month for   years to reach my goal of

You can use the software on our site to do many calculations

instantly.

Example Two:

How much will you accumulate by saving a set amount each month?	
1. What interest rate will you get on your money?	7.5%
2. How many years will you save for?	10 years
3. How much will you save every month?	€400
4. We find the value for 7.5% and ten years on our table..	177.93
5. To find out how much you will accumulate: **We multiply the amount you save each month 400 x 177.93.**	= 71,172

You will have accumulated €71,172 by saving €400 pm for 10 years.

Your money grew at 7.5%
You will save 400 per month and you will save for ten years.
The value from our table was 177.93
You will have a lump sum of €71,172 after ten years.

Your goal sheets help you set goals and stay on target. Winning becomes easier. Your goals change and grow over time. What once seemed impossible becomes second nature to you. These goals will be your goals and not pipe dreams or goals set for you by other people. It's your life and you're in charge. Enjoy and prosper!

Now it's your turn:

How much will you accumulate by saving a set amount each month?	
1. What interest rate will you get on your money?	%
2. How many years will you save for?	years
3. How much will you save every month?	
4. We find the value for interest rate and **years** on our table.	
5. To find out how much you will accumulate: **We multiply the amount you save each month x (rate)**	=

I will have accumulated   by saving   pm
for   **years**

WEALTH BUILDING MIND MAP

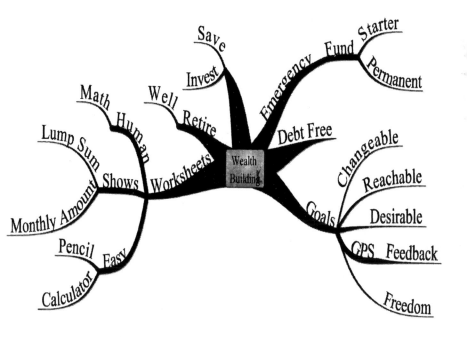

The road to your personal prosperity is here.

Your Wealth Builder Worksheet

We designed this to custom fit your life.

As you progress your priorities change.

Step One: Starter Emergency Fund.

This is the only step that is written in stone, the rest are suggestions.

Many years ago a mentor Pat Howley made suggestions. He ended all suggestions the same way. Pat reminded me that during the Second World War soldiers were asked to pull the rip cord on their parachute, and that too was just a suggestion!

Your Starter Emergency Fund of €1000
Date Accomplished _____

Step Two: Reduce and Remove Debt

You record your progress as a free person. Your goal is to become debt free.

Debt removed the amount is	-	date accomplished	-
Debt payments reduced the amount is	-	date accomplished	-

Step Three: Health Insurance

Maybe you believe that you don't need health insurance, if so you can skip this section. Paying doctors and hospital bills has become America's number one reason for declaring bankruptcy. This is real shock and awe for the rest of us but America has led the way in many areas.

If for no other reason than your quality health care, this is one reason to vote.

What does health insurance really provide? You get quality care without outrageous waiting times; and a choice of providers. Sometimes this is a life and death issue

Health Provider	-	date accomplished	-

Step Four: Three months emergency fund.

This tool gave me the freedom to take time off to write this book.

The emergency fund gave me the freedom to choose where I work. It's a slow and steady accomplishment and you can do it. This step is about freedom. Go for it.

3 months income is	-	date accomplished	-

Step Five: Your Retirement fund.

For the record, we have not opened a traditional pension fund because we agreed to buy our retirement home now. We prefer this action over hoping to trade down later.

Our retirement home has been a complete floor to roof renovation. When completed we will own this home mortgage free. This means that when we retire we can either sell our existing home or else rent it out for additional income.

Can we rent this retirement home? Yes we can rent this as a holiday home, so there were lots of benefits of taking this action first, before we funded a pension.

You must save for your retirement. Your children will have many expenses when you're retired, and they will probably be unable to help. And that doesn't take into account their partner or spouse who will have definite opinions on how they spend!

Once the renovation is completed we'll save in a regular pension. So here goes;

Retirement fund goal	-	date accomplished	-

Step Six: Your children's education fund.

I am assuming that you have children. You help fund their education but only after you have taken care of your basic needs. If you do not save to help towards their education they will probably leave education loaded with student loans.

Again first things first, set a good example, save for your retirement.

Education fund goal	-	date accomplished	-

Step Seven: Your financial freedom.

This is where you have enough saved that you can live off the interest and or dividends. You're working because you want to and not because you have to. You have the freedom to choose your type of work. If you want to volunteer you can.

This is the day where you can choose where you want to live without having to pay a mortgage or the payment is so small that it is insignificant.

A quick and simple way to find out what fund you need to be financially free.

Look at your desired retirement income. Forget your pension for now. Imagine having this income generated from your investments. Now you can retire whenever you want to. This is financial freedom.

You are mortgage free. From our first true income worksheet; you know your true net income. This is your income after tax and work related spending.

Step One Use your true net income:

Enter you true net income from the bottom of that worksheet

_____

Step Two Find the lump sum that you need to be free:

You want to make five per cent on your investments.

Multiply your true net income by 20.
The math is 1 divided by the interest rate, or 1/0.05
This amount is   _____

This is the lump sum that you need to retire from your current work. You do not have to wait for the mandatory age to retire. You create the freedom to choose.

You can redefine retirement to mean volunteer work or work that pays less than you currently earn, for example a corporate lawyer becomes a part time teacher, fulfilling a life long passion to give back and excite the minds of the young.

You can go into much more detail, and finesse the results and outcomes if you want. www.advisordomain.com/book

14

CREATE YOUR FINANCIAL FREEDOM

A mere pipedream for many will become your reality. You can do this!

Look at your desired retirement income. Forget your pension for now. Imagine having this income generated from your investments. Now you can retire whenever you want to. This is financial freedom.

You are mortgage free. From our first worksheet discover your true income; you have found your current true net income. This is your income after tax and work related spending. This is what you actually need to live on. This is the income that you need to replace to achieve financial freedom.

Enter this number now.

Step One

Your true current hourly income is	
Put in the total hours you spend on work	
Multiply your income x the total hours worked each week	
Multiply this by 52	
This is your annual income	
Deduct your mortgage payments from your income, as you are mortgage free Write your annual payment here →	
Deduct your mortgage payment now. This gives us the income you need to replace. this is number **(2)**	

Step Two

How much do I need to have to replace this income?

To live on this income you need to create a lump sum that will do this at 5% interest. Yes you can grow your money at a higher rate but we need to take into account charges such as taxes and mutual fund fees. It is better to be conservative and hit your goal than to be driven by wishful thinking.

To find this sum we now do this:

The lump sum that gives me financial freedom is (2) x 1 / .05
> A shortcut is to multiply your income by 20.

(In case you don't remember 5% is shown as 0.05)

Assume you have a net annual income of 28,000. This is number

(2) from above.

1 divided by 0.05 gives us 20

Multiply 28,000 by 20 gives us 560,000

This means that you need a sum of €560,000 to be

financially free.

If your money grows at 7% per year, you would divide 1 by 0.07=

14.29

Multiplying 28,000 by 14.29 on our trusty calculator gives us

400,120.

This means that you need €400,120 to achieve financial

freedom.

While this seems an easier number to achieve, it is a lofty goal

because you have to pay taxes and fees for growing your money.

You are also assuming wrongly that you will avoid bumps in the

road.

How much do you need in your financial freedom fund?	
1. The income that you want to replace is	€28,000
2. The interest rate that you will get is	7 %
3. Divide 1 by the interest rate (7%) =	14.29
4. Multiply the income by this answer	€400,120

You need to save this sum of money = €400,120

Now it's your turn:

How much do you need in your financial freedom fund?	
1. The income that you want to replace is	
2. The interest rate that you will get is	
3. Divide 1 by the interest rate	
4. Multiply the income by this answer	

You need to save this sum of money =

Important Tip:

To be financially free you need to be mortgage free.

The next best thing is to have a small mortgage payment.

When you prepay your mortgage can you to choose a reducing monthly payment? This means that you keep the same term but every time you make an extra payment your normal mortgage payment is reduced. It takes time to see a difference but it is very exciting!

Healthy Money Tip
For self employed people or anyone whose income can vary I think that this is a better route. The lower your monthly payments the easier it is to be free

Follow these simple steps and you can achieve this goal of being mortgage free.

Ask your lender how many years will you knock off your mortgage if you pay an extra €5 per week? Ask and you will be amazed. Alternatively you can use our software found at www.advisordomain.com

Part Four

Mortgages, How to master your mortgage

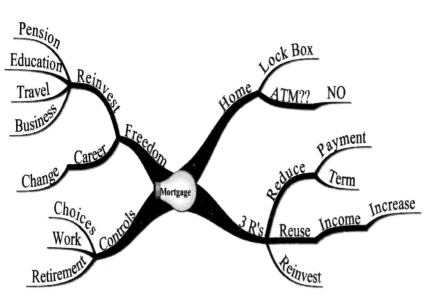

Mortgage Mind Map

Put your home in a lock box.

I

Mortgage Rule Number One

WARNING: Nobody but nobody should have access to your lockbox without your considered permission.

Your home is your most important asset. Your home payment is your most important expense. Keep this expense as low as possible. Your mortgage costs more than your home.

Banks know that you will do anything to keep your home that is why they will let you borrow against your home. Your home is not your personal ATM.

When you borrow against your home you put it at risk. Sometimes you are so overwhelmed with personal debts that you will have to. If you have to do this is there any way for you not to put all of your personal loans on your mortgage?

One of the great lies and fallacies that we have all been told is that the rich borrow against their homes to create more wealth. This is simply not true, and there is no, and I mean NO evidence that backs up this nonsensical claim.

When you borrow against your home to invest in an *"appreciating asset"*, this works only if the asset you have invested in continues to go up in value.

In a time of rising tides this can make you look smart. But when the tide goes out as it inevitably will, you face ruin. You face falling real estate values, falling rents, no tenants, rising interest rate costs, and worst of all no get out of jail clause.

Here is my alternative wealth building proposition:

When your mortgage is gone, you can stop working or you can use your mortgage payment to build up a huge savings fund.

2

Should you repay your mortgage early?

- Healthy money means that you strive to be mortgage free

- Your mortgage is your largest monthly expense, with it gone you have taken a huge step to financial freedom.

- Until you have paid off your mortgage you will probably have to work.

- Until you repay your mortgage your lender is a silent monkey on your back.

What is the best action to pay off your mortgage early?

There is one simple action above all others that will knock years off your mortgage.

- Make one extra payment every year.

So the question is how do you make one extra payment per year?

My current mortgage payment is   _____

This payment divided by two is   _____

This is the payment that you make twice a year to knock up to 8 years off a 30 year mortgage at 5 % interest; at 6% you will knock 5 ½ years off.

Divide this payment by 6. This will give you the amount you need to save each month   _____

Can you create at least 5 ways that you can save this money?
For example coins in a jar, you are paid every two weeks and you will use the third payment twice a year to make this extra payment.

1. _____

2. _____

3. _____

4. _____

5. _____

Why do you want to do this?

_____

_____

What would it feel like to be mortgage free?

_____

_____

_____

Are you willing to commit to the goal
of being mortgage free?   _____

Important Mortgage Tip:

If you have a variable income you should work on reducing your

mortgage payment instead of reducing your mortgage term.

If you have a commission based income or if you are self em-

ployed you should work on reducing your monthly payment. **If**

times are hard it is more important to have a smaller monthly

payment than a reduced term.

In other words when you make an extra payment you choose

to either reduce your mortgage term or your mortgage pay-

ment.

For example you make a lump sum payment and you can

reduce your term by three years or you can reduce your monthly

payment by €100 a month you are smarter to reduce your payment. If your income drops during hard times you will be better

off. A smaller payment means less stress.

3

DOES IT MAKE SENSE FOR YOU TO RE-MORTGAGE?

As a mortgage specialist I have found that there are three main reasons that you will re-mortgage;

1. You want to get a lower interest rate on your loan.

2. You want to consolidate your loans into one single payment.

3. You want to release equity from your home. This cash can be used for any purpose from going on vacation to investing in your business or real estate.

The re-mortgage planner worksheet allows you to compare where you are and decide if it makes sense for you to re-mortgage.

Basically you have a monthly payment today and you will have a new payment after re-mortgaging. You will have fees and costs in re-mortgaging so how many months will it take you to breakeven?

Item six asks you to fill in your monthly payment, if you are consolidating your debts you could fill in your total monthly payments.

Important:

1.   When you consolidate your loans into your mortgage you are taking debt that is unsecured and securing it against your home. Think before you do this. If things go wrong you may lose your home.

2.   Ask your mortgage broker to give you a true cost of credit comparison. This compares the total amount of interest that you will pay by remortgaging versus staying as you are.

3.   If at all possible shorten your mortgage term. This means that you will not only pay less each month but that you will pay the banks for fewer months.

4.   Set a goal to become mortgage free; and to use your mortgage payment to boost your retirement or financial freedom savings.

5.   In an ideal world you should not consolidate to lower your monthly payments but high monthly loan payments will destroy good relationships. Often if you have high interest loans you will actually pay less by consolidating.

6. Ask your lender how much freedom you have with this loan. So you ask:

- Can you prepay without penalty?

- Can you shorten the term with prepayments?

- Can you reduce your monthly payment by making extra payments?

- Can you take a payment holiday? If you lost your job this is a very important benefit to have.

- Can you go interest only? For the same reason as above this is a great benefit. If this is part of the lender's package you only need to make a simple phone call rather than having to negotiate.

- If your mortgage is not fixed can you fix it in the future?

The goal of this planner is to help you save money on your largest expense.

Go through it step by step, you will find it easy to do.

4

REMORTGAGE MIND MAP

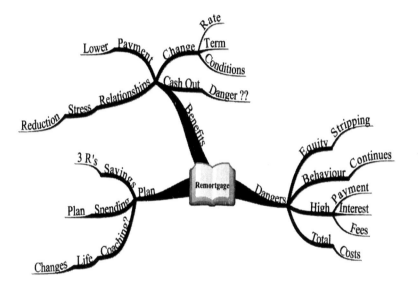

5

TEN STEPS TO A PROFITABLE RE-MORTGAGE

You want to get an apple to apples comparison. So we use the same mortgage amount, the same term, and add any loan fees or costs to this amount. If you are borrowing more that is okay but for now we want to compare apples to apples.

This is easy to do, just fill in the blanks on the right. Questions four and five are not vital for now. You can compare for now with the answers to six and seven.

Quick Start Refinancing Quiz	
1. What is your home worth today?	
2. What is the balance on your mortgage?	
3. What is the loan to value on your home? (2÷1) divide the answer in step two by the value of your home in step one.	
4. What is your current interest rate today? (This is for the purists. It is not absolutely necessary right now. You can get this later).	
5. What is the best available interest rate that you qualify for?	
6. What is your current monthly payment?	
7. What would your new monthly payment be?	
8. How much will you save every month by refinancing? (7-6) What is the difference between your old and new payment?	
9. What are your costs for refinancing?	
10. **How many months will it take you to breakeven?** (9÷8) We divide your costs of refinancing (step nine) by your monthly savings in step eight.	

Is this worth it? Are you comparing like with like?

For example;

- Does either mortgage have a prepayment penalty?
- Does either mortgage have late payment fees? Are they the same?
- Which loan has a lower APR? Your broker or lender can tell you this. The lower the APR the better.
- Are there any special features on either mortgage? Such as
- Payment holidays. This is where you can take a break from making payments.
- How do other people rate the service departments of the lenders? Some lenders are very harsh if you fall behind. Your current lender may be very easy to work with, so this is important information.
- Will either lender allow you to go interest only? If times ever became hard this could be a very important option.
- Ask your new lender why this is a smart money move for you?

Here is a Super Mega Money Making Tip. No Kidding!

Tell your existing lender that you intend to move. Ask them what can they offer you to stay? Most lenders are intelligent. They will improve your current deal. This one tip is worth the price of this book many times over.

6

HOW MUCH WILL MY MORTGAGE COST?

Monthly repayment chart – cost per €1,000 borrowed.

Rate %	5	10	15	20	25	30	35
3.25	18.08	9.77	7.03	5.67	4.87	4.35	3.99
3.5	18.19	9.89	7.15	5.80	5.01	4.49	4.13
3.75	18.30	10.01	7.27	5.93	5.14	4.63	4.28
4.0	18.42	10.12	7.40	6.06	5.28	4.77	4.43
4.25	18.53	10.24	7.52	6.19	5.42	4.92	4.58
4.5	18.64	10.36	7.65	6.33	5.56	5.07	4.73
4.75	18.76	10.48	7.78	6.46	5.70	5.22	4.89
5.0	18.87	10.61	7.91	6.60	5.85	5.37	5.05
5.25	18.99	10.73	8.04	6.74	5.99	5.52	5.21
5.5	19.10	10.85	8.17	6.88	6.14	5.68	5.37

5.75	19.22	10.98	8.30	7.02	6.29	5.84	5.54
6.0	19.33	11.10	8.44	7.16	**6.44**	6.00	5.70
6.25	19.45	11.23	8.57	7.31	6.60	6.16	5.87
6.5	19.57	11.35	8.71	7.46	6.75	6.32	6.04
6.75	19.68	11.48	8.85	7.60	6.91	6.49	6.21
7.0	19.80	11.61	8.99	7.75	7.07	6.65	6.39
7.25	19.92	11.74	9.13	7.90	7.23	6.82	6.56
7.5	20.04	11.87	9.27	8.06	7.39	6.99	6.74
7.75	20.16	12.00	9.41	8.21	7.55	7.16	6.92
8.0	20.28	12.13	9.56	8.36	7.72	7.34	7.10
8.25	20.40	12.27	9.70	8.52	7.88	7.51	7.28
8.5	20.52	12.40	9.85	8.68	8.05	7.69	7.47
8.75	20.64	12.53	9.99	8.84	8.22	7.87	7.65
9.0	20.76	12.67	10.14	9.00	8.39	8.05	7.84
9.25	20.88	12.80	10.29	9.16	8.56	8.23	8.03
9.5	21.00	12.94	10.59	9.49	8.91	8.59	8.41
9.75	21.25	13.08	10.75	9.65	9.09	8.78	8.60

10	21.25	13.22	10.75	9.65	9.09	8.78	8.60
10.25	21.37	13.35	10.90	9.82	9.26	8.96	8.79
10.5	21.49	13.49	11.05	9.98	9.44	9.15	8.98
10.75	21.62	13.63	11.21	10.15	9.62	9.33	9.18
11	21.74	13.78	11.37	10.32	9.80	9.52	9.37
11.25	21.87	13.92	11.52	10.49	9.98	9.71	9.56

A simple example:

You have a mortgage of €200,000

Your interest rate is 6%

Your mortgage term is 25 years.

On the chart above we see that the rate is 6.44 per thousand.

Our calculator multiplies 200 by 6.44 =1288. You pay €1,288 per month for 25 yrs.

Mortgage Coaching

Do you want to get the best deal on your mortgage? The best deal can save you thousands and knock years off your mortgage. For readers living in Ireland this is what you can achieve with mortgage coaching and a follow up plan of action:

- Should you have a fixed or variable rate mortgage. The emotional reasons are often more important than the actual rates. *The best variable rate mortgage is useless if it keeps you awake at night worrying over rising interest rates.*

- Find out what is the lowest rate mortgage that you will actually qualify for. There is no point in applying for a mortgage that you will not get.

- What are the potential savings if you re-mortgage?

- What is the true cost comparison of staying put versus moving for a better deal? Sometimes it makes no sense to move to a lower rate mortgage. The costs of remortgaging outweigh the benefits.

How much does this cost?

Contact me for details.

Do I need to do the mortgage through you?

No you can work with anyone. We want to explore all options which include staying with your current lender, and yes your broker can do any new mortgage.

What is the ultimate goal of this coaching session?

As your coach I want to give you a plan of action that will help you save thousands and knock years off your mortgage. Being mortgage free is an important part of being financially free.

PART FIVE

YOUR KEYS TO CREATING A PROSPEROUS RETIREMENT

If you are lucky you will retire and grow old. You face challenges hugely different from your grandparents such as living longer, health care and assisted living.

Today you may be stressed out with all of the challenges that you face, but you have an enormous advantage. You can work more, work smarter, and change your career or business, move city, country, lifestyle. When you retire you will lose many of these options that you now take for granted.

It's heartbreaking to see people struggle in retirement. You can be different. Start today. It is not too late for you to vastly improve the quality of your retirement.

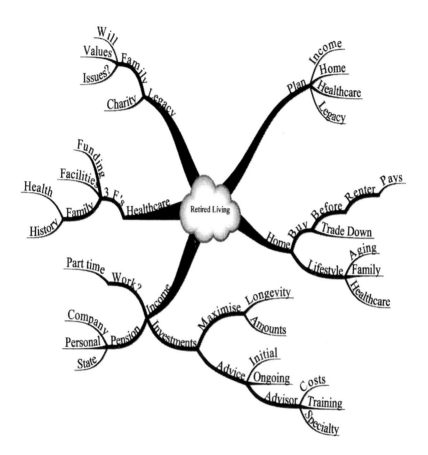

Retired living mind map

I

A Tale of Three Retirements

The people who were my mentors had something great about the way they lived. You won't find their work in a bookstore or recorded in history. Yet they lived their lives with serenity and joy. As a pebble leaves a ripple when thrown into the pond, this manual is the ripple of all that they shared.

When I was in my last year of University I met Tom. When the student is ready the teacher appears. Tom was an intellectual who lived a diverse full life on his terms. This gave him great freedom.

We all have family stories that impact us greatly.
Tom told me the story of his father. He saved his entire life and looked forward to the day he retired. The day after he retired Tom's father died. The next day Tom's mother went out and

bought a new car. Ireland at this time was at best an austere country. After a life of penny pinching Tom's mother wanted a taste of luxury.

What Tom learnt from this is that you must live for today with joy.

Don't postpone joy for that time when you are no longer working. This was a prescient lesson because Tom died before he retired. His life had an incredible impact on mine. Tom taught me that you do not need to go to University to learn, you do not need to be religious to be spiritual. To seek God without religion is much harder and probably more fulfilling.

My own father had misgivings about saving for a pension. As an accountant he saw the devastating effects of inflation on a fixed pension. In those days you saved all your life and handed over the money to an insurance company who gave you an income for life. If you died early you wife got a much smaller income.

My father had the wrong idea from this; he could not see the point of saving for something that could be diminished to the point of nothingness. So my dad only started to save late in his working life.

He figured if he put all his energy into building a professional practice that this would be his pension. Basically this is good advice but that is not how it worked out. My father died a month before his 65th birthday. As he had technically retired to take up a new post his partners said he no longer had equity in the practice which he helped build up.

- This is what I have learned. People with money have more options. This is most obviously true for retired people.

For you and I who are still working we have a get out of jail clause. If we are in financial difficulty we can somehow increase our income. We can get a new job, a second job, a part time business or even get a raise.

For the first time in history ordinary homeowners have a get out of jail card, and that is their home. You can sell it and trade down, borrow against it with a reverse mortgage, or sell a piece of it to an investor.

We live in the time of prosperity that has never been seen before. Prosperity has been achieved by a greater percentage of ordinary people than ever before. But we can never forecast today's prosperity as being fixed like a star in the sky.

You could retire in a time of war. You could retire in a time of great economic hardship. And you could be lucky and retire in a time of plenty.

When times were hard retirees faired poorly. They got little of what was there to be shared. When planning for your retirement it is wise to assume the worst.

When you are retired you will still want to experience joy. You do not wake up on the day that you are retired saying "I am ready for a life of less than".

Our healthy retirement planner helps you create the retirement that you want and not the retirement that we pension sellers want you to buy. We want you to aspire for more because we make more money this way. We can pretend that we want you to have more and lots more from a noble perspective but why should we pretend?

So where should we go from here?

- We make a realistic plan for our retirement based on our goals, desires and our current true net income. We get this from your true income worksheet.
- You have a lot more options than you may be aware of.
- Life is easier when we plan.
- Anything extra that you can have when retired is a bonus.
- Health care is going to be a major issue for all of us when we retire.
- We want to have the extra options that come from having money.
- If you work when you are retired it will be because you want to work and not because you have to work.
- Your desire to be a free human being will always be there.
- Saving today means that you have learnt to live on less than you earn. This is a good habit to bring into your retirement.

Here is a simple task for you:

Look at people you know who are retired and ask yourself; "would their lives be easier if they had a little extra money?" €500 extra per month may not seem like much to you or I but it could be huge to a retired person. Change this €500 number so that it makes sense for your life.

I am saying this simply for the person who thinks that it is too late to save. I want to point out that you still have time to make a big difference to your retirement.

2

YOUR GOAL FOR A RETIREMENT FUND

When you retire, you will have to decide what to do with your retirement fund. This will be an enormous decision, and it is best to plan ahead of time. You need an advisor to help you create a pension with maximum options.

In Ireland you are allowed to take one quarter of your fund as a tax free lump sum. The balance is invested in a fund that is designed to give you a lifetime income.

You are allowed to put this money into a fund that you can control. Sadly, some pensions do not have this option. To get this option for all people you need to vote. Only politicians can change the legislation on equal pension options for all citizens. Vote.

Like everything else with control comes responsibility. You face the risk of being left in a terrible situation living hand to mouth if you make poor investment decisions.

When you retire you will not have a personality change. So by learning to make wise decisions today, you will be able to make wise decisions tomorrow.

Having control of your pension fund, after retirement, allows you to create more healthy financial freedom. The fund is yours, and what is not spent is given to your estate.

In the old days you simply bought an annuity. This gave you an income for life, a reduced income for your spouse. And when you died the money was gone. Yes there were variations but the principle was that you no longer owned the retirement fund, this died with you.

You'll need a great financial advisor by your side, so the time to find the right one is today. This is a different topic to the one that I want to discuss with you now.

- All over the western world we are all living longer and working longer.

- Here is an alternative way to control your pension fund.

Below are the steps to see where you will stand. After this I will show you a simple example. We are not looking for exactitude your advisor can be very specific. We just want to see the broad lay of the land.

Step One

When I retire I will have a retirement fund of	

(You can get this projected information from your advisor or fund company).

Step Two

Divide this fund by four to get your tax free lump sum	

Step Three

Divide this number by five to get an annual income for five years	

Step Four

What is the balance of your retirement fund for a pension?	

By using your lump sum for the first five years you continue to grow the balance of your fund. This changes your time horizon for when you need the money. The longer the investment term you have to invest the more risk you can take.

I am not suggesting that all of your money be put into risky investments, just that a bigger portion can be used as long term investments for a better return.

There are two keys to successful investment returns, one is asset allocation and the second is having a system. When you retire there will be fantastic technology to help you and your advisor make wise asset allocation decisions.

If you desire to work part time then your lump sum income makes this doable.

For example:

When I retire I will have a retirement fund of	€200,000
Divide this fund by four to get your tax free lump sum	€50,000
Divide this number by five to get an annual income for five years	€10,000

This gives you an income of close to €200 per week. Can you work part time or even do volunteer work?

What is the balance of your retirement fund used for a pension	€150,000

Supposing you want to work part time for a non profit organisation and your income from this would be €250 per week.

Your income is now €450 per week. That is €200 from your lump sum and a wage of €250 per week. I have assumed that you get no interest on your money.

Will this allow you to work part time? Remember by now your home is free and clear. As you do the other exercises you will see if this is enough for you.

1. One alternative is to use the remaining €150,000 to get you an extra income.

2. Another choice would be to delay retirement by one year.

3. A third choice is to boost your retirement savings.

3

How you plan for a comfortable retirement

We are going to use the retirement creator worksheet.

Normally when we sell pension planning we tell you that you need massive amounts of money. When you agree we make more money as advisors because we have more money invested. Like everyone else we are paid on results.

Like every other advisor I want to be successful, and this is where we are potentially if not fatally in conflict with our clients. No one gets paid a bonus for saying I told our clients not to invest any more, they have plenty, stop investing and go away for a nice break.

Everyone, from the butcher to the baker makes money when you buy. The farmer makes money when you buy his produce or if he can convince the government that he should get free money. Free money for him is called a subsidy.

The investment advisor makes money from the sale of advice and from the sale of products. If we are paid in any way by the size of your portfolio then we have a vested interest in your growing that fund. Put more in is the simplest growth strategy. A client with a growing portfolio is a client who'll pay for advice.

The best tool of all for the wealthy client is to play the fear card. Now that you have it why should you lose it? I don't want to lose it, do you?

What I want is for you to say what would be a comfortable retirement lifestyle. To get to this I want you to cut away all the expenses you will no longer have.

For example if you no longer have a mortgage payment of €1,500 per month why would you save to replace? If you have been funding your children's education by another €500 per month then again why would you save to replace this income?

My own view is that you should finish your mortgage early while also saving for your retirement. When your mortgage is finished put this towards your pension.

Your goal is to avoid a miserly retired existence, and to avoid being crucified by saving for retirement. *You get a separate tool for funding your retirement home before you retire, as this is a huge benefit.* Every tool is interlinked to help you succeed.

4

YOUR RIGHT SIZED RETIREMENT FUND CREATOR

What we are asking here is how much will you need to retire comfortably?

Step One

What is your current monthly income after taxes?	
We are going to deduct the following expenses from your after tax income. You will not have these expenses when you retire.	
1. Mortgage Payment (you own your home free and clear)	
2. Your current Pension contributions	
3. Your work related expenses	
4. Children's education expenses	
5. Other	

6. Other	
7. Other	
8. Other	
9. Other	
10. Other	
We add all of these expenses which will disappear on retirement.	

Some of these are listed and you have space to add expenses.

Step Two

We are going to find out how much you need each month.

Your current net monthly income is	
We deduct your expenses from step 1.	
This will give us the monthly income that you really need	

Step Three

We want to see what your funding shortfall is.

We are going to take your other pensions and government benefits into account.

You have an existing projected pension of	

(This would come from a pension at work, or from a previous employer. You can also use your own retirement savings here.)

Your projected government/State pension is	
We add these two pensions	
From step 2 you need an income of	
Deduct the income from your existing pensions	
This gives us the monthly income that you need to replace	

Step Four

What is your life expectancy after you retire?

At the back of the book we have a life expectancy table. This will tell you how long you can expect to live after you retire.

I want to retire at age	
I can expect to live until age	
The difference between the two is	

This is the number of years that you will be retired for.

Step Five

How much do you need in a retirement fund to generate this income?

We take the monthly income you need and multiply it by 12	

We multiply your annual income by the number of years you are retired for. (We got this from step four)	

This is the total amount that you need to have in savings.

We are making some silly assumptions.

Example:

You need a monthly income of €3,000 per month.

This gives you an annual income of €36,000

Your life expectancy is 18 years, multiply by €36,000 and you need €648,000.

We are assuming that you give yourself the same amount of money each month. So if you get €3,000 per month you get this in month one and it never changes for the rest of your life. Inflation would destroy your monthly income. Your real income might drop from €3,000 down to €1,000 per month because of inflation.

We are assuming that your retirement fund does not grow at all. Again this is a silly assumption. These two assumptions allow us to get a working number you aim for.

Here is the table that will help you save the right amount of money

Interest Rate	Years until retirement						
	1	5	10	15	20	30	40
2.5 %	12.14	63.84	136.17	218.12	310.97	535.37	823.46
5.0 %	12.28	68.01	155.28	267.29	411.03	832.26	1526.02

7.5 %	12.42	72.53	177.93	331.11	**553.73**	1347.45	3023.82
10.0 %	12.57	77.44	204.84	414.47	759.37	2260.49	6324.08

Step Seven

Find out how much you need to save.	
1. How many years do you have until you retire?	20 years
2. We assume that your money will grow by 7.5% a year	7.5%
You get a value from the table above	**553.73**
3. Divide the sum you need, 648,000 by the factor 553.73 from the table above.	
4. We divide €648,000 by the factor 554 and we get	1169.68

This means that you need to save €1170 every month to get €648,000
If you haven't saved this can be a very scary number!

Look at a younger person's outlook.	
Let's assume that you are young and you have forty years to save.	(we get 3023.82)
5. If we divide €648,000 by 3024 we get	214.36.

So with 40 years you only need to save €214 per month!

Now it's your turn.
Use the table and fill in the blank boxes below.

Find out how much you need to save.	

1. How many years do you have until you retire?	
2. What percentage will you expect your money to grow by?	%
3. You get a value from the table above and enter	
4. Divide the sum you need, by the factor from the table.	
We divide € by and we get -	

This means that you need to save €   every month
to get €   ,000

So you have two factors. One is the growth or interest rate, and

the second is time.

You pick the rate that you think your money will grow at.

Try this exercise, it is very easy.
- See what happens at a higher and lower rate of growth.
- See what happens when you delay retirement by five years.

Here is a rule of thumb; the longer your investment time period;

the higher the rate of growth that you can aim for with your

money.

This is because you can invest more of your money in higher risk investments which provide higher returns. A younger person can wait out a stock market crash.

This is why I am recommending that you buy your retirement home before you retire. You can sell it to boost your fund, and you may be able to borrow against it. This may not be possible if times are hard, and interest rates are high.

Let me be clear. Do not buy your retirement home through your pension. There may be tax advantages to this but they can change. You have put all of your eggs in one basket. Your pension and retirement home are all interlinked.

Healthy Money Tip

If you can live off one quarter of your fund for five years, this changes your outlook. This allows you to take a ten year investment outlook on some of your retirement fund. You will not need your entire fund at the end of the five years.

On the next page we will go through an example step by step.

5

YOUR RIGHT SIZED RETIREMENT FUND CREATOR

█ A step by step example

What we are asking here is how much will you need to retire comfortably?

Step One

What is your current monthly income after taxes?	€5,750

Step Two

We want to remove all of your current expenses that you will not

have when you retire. Some of these are listed but you have space

to add expenses from your current lifestyle.

We are going to deduct the following expenses from your after

tax income.

Mortgage Payment (you own your home free and clear)	€1,100

Your current Pension contributions	€300
Your work related expenses (use the net monthly income work sheet to get this number.)	€376
Children's education expenses (from fees to accommodation)	€175
Other car loan payments on high end car. You will change your car less often when you retire.	€440
Home renovation loan payment	€315
Other	€0
We add all of the expenses which will disappear on retirement.	€2706

Step Three

We are going to find out how much you need each month.

Your current net monthly income is	€5750
We deduct your expenses from step 2.	€2706
This will give us the monthly income that you really need	€3,044

Step Four

We want to see what your shortfall is
We are going to take your other pensions and government benefits into account.

You have an existing projected pension of	€0

(This comes from a pension at work, or a previous employer. You can also use your own retirement savings here.)

Your projected State pension is	€840
We add these two pensions	€840
From step 3 you need an income of	€3044
Deduct the income from your existing pensions	€840
This gives us the monthly income that you need to replace	€2204

Step Five

How much will you need in a retirement fund to generate this income?

At the back of the book use the life expectancy table. This will tell you how long you can expect to live after you retire.

1. I want to retire at age   65
2. I can expect to live until age   87
3. The difference between the two is 22 years.
This is the number of years that you will be retired for.

Step Six

We take the monthly income you need €2204 and multiply it by twelve. €26,446

We multiply your annual income by the number of years (22) you are retired for €581,856

This is the total amount that you need to have in savings. **Again this is €581,856**

We are making some silly assumptions.

Example:

You need a monthly income of €2,204 per month.

This gives you an annual income of €26,446

Your life expectancy is 22 years, multiply this by €26,446 and you need €581,856 in your retirement fund.

We are assuming that you give yourself the same amount of money each month. So if you get €2,204 per month you get this in month one and it never changes for the rest of your life. Inflation would destroy your monthly income. Here your real income might drop from €2,204 all the way down to €700 per month because of inflation.

We are assuming that your retirement fund does not grow at all. Again this is a silly assumption. These two assumptions allow us to get a working number that you can aim for.

Step Seven

Find out how much you need to save.

How many years do you have until you retire? You are 45 so you have **20 years to save**

For example we will assume that you have 20 working years until you retire.

Get a value from the table below

Divide the sum you need, say €581,586 by the factor from the table.

We are going to assume that you will grow your money by **7.5% per year.**

If we look at the table below under 20 years at 7.5% we see that the number is **553.73**

So we take the fund we need €581,586 and divide it by **554** and we get **1,049.79.** This means that you need to save **€1050** every month to reach your goal.

If you haven't saved this can be a very scary number.

Let's assume that you are young and you have forty years to save.

If we look at the table we get 3023.82

If we divide €581,586 by 3024 we get **192.32. So you only need to save €192 per month!**

This is why I am recommending that you buy your retirement home before you retire. This means you can use your current home as a rental property giving you an extra income. You can sell it to boost your fund, and you may be able to borrow against it. This may not be possible if times are hard, and interest rates are high.

Let me be clear. I am not recommending that you buy your retirement home through your pension. There are tax advantages to this when you rent the home until you retire but I think that you have put all of your eggs in one basket. In reality your pension and retirement home are all interlinked.

If you can live off one quarter of your fund for five years, this can change your outlook. This allows you to take a ten year investment outlook on some of your retirement fund. You will not need your entire fund after five years.

Here is the table that will help you save the right amount of money

Interest Rate	Years until retirement						
	1	5	10	15	20	30	40
2.5 %	12.14	63.84	136.17	218.12	310.97	535.37	823.46
5.0 %	12.28	68.01	155.28	267.29	411.03	832.26	1526.02
7.5 %	12.42	72.53	177.93	331.11	553.73	1347.45	3023.82
10.0 %	12.57	77.44	204.84	414.47	759.37	2260.49	6324.08

6

THE WORLD'S BEST WAY TO START A PENSION

Here is the simplest tool to create your healthy pension.

▌ **Take a baby step.**

My goal is to help you starting today to create an abundant pension. We all know that we should save 15% of our income. This is easy to say but very difficult to do.

This system works. It works for everyone in just about every circumstance.

We start by taking baby steps.

You have reduced or removed your personal loans. You may be in a position to reduce your debts and at the same time save for a pension. While our goal is to be debt free save for a pension if you can. Pensions have fantastic tax benefits.

Remember that the principles that we share are universal, the details are local.

So in your country the tax benefits may be different than mine

but the principles of healthy money are the same.

Here are my assumptions about you:

- Starting from today you can save 2% of your income.

- Every year you get a pay raise. If you get no pay raise in any given year, you are in a holding position. You do not take the next step.

- I am assuming that you get a pay raise of 4% each year.

- When you get a pay raise, you increase your savings by 2% of your income.

- This means that each increase is painless because you increase your savings from money that you have not yet seen.

- When you get to saving 15% of your income you can stop if you wish.

- As your debts are removed from your life this makes this much easier to do.

What happens if I don't get a pay raise?

Our goal is to increase your savings only as your income increases. In this year you do not increase your savings.

What if I just can't afford to increase my savings by 2% each time I get a pay raise?

You need to be honest with yourself. Are you spending your raise on extra goodies or on necessities? If you need the money for basics then by all means increase your savings by only 1%, or even a half of a per cent. When times are tough you may put increases on the shelf. Your issue here is how do I increase my income?

I'm self employed, does this work for me?

This works brilliantly for the self employed. You save more as your income grows.

I can save more than 2% to start, is that okay?

Yes, this is wonderful. Our goal is to get you to save 15% so the quicker we get there the better. Our goal is to make this painless, so if each step is a baby step you will stick to this program and prosper.

On the next page you can see what happens if you follow this simple program.

We assumed that:

- You started saving 2% of your income.

- You increased your income by 4% a year.

- You increased your pension savings by 2% a year.

- When you got to saving 15% a year you stayed at this level every year.

- Your money grew by 6% a year. Anything better is used to offset inflation.

What happens when you retire?

You'll live in a home that you chose. You can choose to sell or rent your home instead of having to trade down.

You will be mortgage free.

You have lived on less than you earn and this gives great freedom when you retire.

Your pension was created painlessly, and has replaced your true income.

As you face into your retirement years you will have both income and assets to help you get long term care. As I look at my mother who needs long term care, I can see that this is vitally important. Look at your own family and friends. Is this an important issue for you?

7

THE EASY RETIREMENT PLANNER
(FOR LATE BLOOMERS)

We have two examples of people saving 2% per year.

For a calculator to personalise this go to

www.advisordomain.com

Example One

You start by saving 2% and you increase by 2% a year.

Your Starting Income Today	€50,000
Average Annual Raise	4%
Starting Percentage saved for retirement fund	2%
Savings Percentage Increase per year	2%
Maximum percentage of income you will save	15%
Number of years you have to save	30
Interest or growth rate you get	6%

Total lump sum you will have accumulated	€809,336

Source: Gerard Malone. For illustration purposes only

As you can see a small start can blossom into a secure retirement.

Example 2

Here you start late, and you have only five years to save.
You start by saving 2% a year and you increase by 2% per year as you get a raise.

Your Starting Income Today	€40,000
Average Annual Raise	4%
Starting Percentage saved for retirement fund	2%
Savings Percentage Increase per year	3%
Maximum percentage of income you will save	15%
Number of years you have to save	5
Interest or growth rate you get	6%
Total lump sum you will have accumulated	€24,552

Source: Gerard Malone. For illustration purposes only

8

RETIREMENT EXAMPLE WHERE YOU START AT 2% OF YOUR INCOME

Year	Your Monthly Income	Monthly Savings	% Saved	Total Saved
1	4167	83	2%	1,028
2	4333	173	4%	3,226
3	4507	270	6%	6,754
4	4687	375	8%	11,782
5	4874	487	10%	18,499
6	5069	608	12%	27,110
7	5272	738	14%	37,838
8	5483	822	15%	50,249
9	5702	855	15%	63,810
10	5930	890	15%	78,607

Year	Your Monthly Income	Monthly Savings	% Saved	Total Saved
11	6168	925	15%	94,731
12	6414	962	15%	112,278
13	6671	1001	15%	131,353
14	6938	1041	15%	152,065
15	7215	1082	15%	174,534
16	7504	1126	15%	198,884
17	7804	1171	15%	225,251
18	8116	1217	15%	253,777
19	8441	1266	15%	284,615
20	8779	1317	15%	317,928
21	9130	1369	15%	353,889
22	9495	1424	15%	392,683
23	9875	1481	15%	434,507
24	10270	1540	15%	479,572
25	10680	1602	15%	528,099

Year	Your Monthly Income	Monthly Savings	% Saved	Total Saved
26	11108	1666	15%	580,329
27	11552	1733	15%	636,514
28	12014	1802	15%	696,925
29	12495	1874	15%	761,849
30	12994	1949	15%	831,593

Source: Gerard Malone. For illustration purposes only

We have made some simple assumptions:

1. You get a raise of 4% every year. Obviously life doesn't work this way, your circumstances may be very different, but it is a good start.

2. You are able to save every year. In other words life doesn't get in the way. You will have unusual expenses like medical care, educational fees for your children, nursing home fees for your parents, a mortgage for your self. We ignored these expenses.

3. Your money grows by 6% every year, some years this would be laughably small and in other years a 10% loss might be a good result. This is not the place to introduce variable returns; our website will do this in the future. You need high powered software to show these variances.

4. At no stage did you use a lump sum to increase to retirement funds. These can come from bonuses; a sale of other investments where you reinvest in a pension, or possibly an inheritance.

Our goals are simple:

- You want to start small. You begin by saving 2% of your monthly Income.

- You increase your savings by 2% each year as your income increases.

- If you get no increase in your income, you can stay at your current level, until your income increases again.
- Your goal is to save 15% of your income, we stop at 15%.

- Your money has grown at 6% per year after all expenses.

9

WHERE WILL YOU LIVE WHEN YOU RETIRE?

Today real estate is falling all over the world just a short while ago it was booming. It is easy to assume that the good times will be here when we retire. Today if you are retired you have many options with your home. You can get a reverse mortgage, you can sell equity in your home or you can sell and trade down.

These options may not be available when you retire.

Wouldn't it be a lot easier to have your ideal retirement home bought? This means you can use your existing home for a rental income or you can sell it for the cash. If you rent, you have a valuable asset to pass on to your children or grandchildren.

If you accept the idea that you will not spend your retirement in your existing home then this makes sense. Many of my clients want to live in the same area but in a smaller home which is more manageable.

A growing area of concern for all of us is long term care when we are elderly.

How will you pay for this? For me this is another reason to plan ahead. Today if you have a reverse mortgage and you go to a nursing home you may be forced to either sell your home or to pay off the mortgage. So please don't assume that your equity in your home or the government will take care of you.

The worksheet takes you through the process of buying your retirement home while you're working. Get a renter to help you buy your home and plan on upgrading your home before you move in.

What happens if you get the tenant from hell? You plan on having 6 months of your mortgage payments in a savings account. The tenant from hell generally wrecks the place as well as stiffing you on the rent.

You can go to seminars or read books on real estate. They're the experts, I don't pretend to be. But I've done this, and I can tell you it gives you an enormous sense of freedom.

So let's get started.

Or is this one of the great ideas that you put on the shelf?

YOUR RETIREMENT HOME PLANNER

Where would you like to live when you retire?

_____

We are looking for the area or type of location, for example by the sea on the east coast. Think of an area that has good amenities, a quality health care system. Is it important that this area is easy for friends and relatives to visit?

_____

_____

_____

_____

Will you trade down to buy this home?

_____

If you or your partner had to go to a nursing home how would

you pay for it? Economic circumstances can change very quickly.

History records countless times when people and nations moved

from feast to famine in a short period of time. So please don't assume that if there is plenty of help for retirees today that you will get the same benefits.

One solution is to buy your ideal retirement home before you retire. The idea is that you rent it, and use the rent to help you buy it.

Here is how we work out if you can do this.

1. What would this home cost today?	
2. How much can you pay down as a deposit?	

The larger your deposit, the less you borrow and the lower your monthly payment.

How long a mortgage term can you get?	

This is the rule; the longer your mortgage term; the lower your monthly payment. You also pay more interest with a longer term.

What are your loan and legal fees for this transaction?	
How much would it cost to furnish this property?	

If you're going to use this as a holiday home in the summer, you need to furnish it. Will you have to furnish it? Interior decoration costs and should be factored in.

How much will you borrow the money for the decoration?	

You get this figure by adding all of the monies you need to borrow. Get quotes. Unless you're buying today a good faith estimate of your costs will work for now.

How much will your mortgage cost you each month?	
If interest rates rose by 2% what would your mortgage cost?	

If your mortgage rate can fluctuate you need to plan for the worst. You do this by seeing if you can afford a mortgage at a much higher rate of interest.

Will you rent this property?	
How much would you get in rent each month?	

- It's smart to assume that your home will be vacant at least one month a year

Your monthly mortgage costs are	
Your monthly insurance costs are	
Your monthly maintenance costs are	
Your total costs are	
Your rent is	
What is the profit or loss?	
If this is a loss can you afford this?	

Can you pay all costs if you've no tenant for 6 months?	
Can you put 3 months of your mortgage and maintenance costs in a special rainy day account?	

Simple Tips:

- Consider buying a site. When the site has been paid for, build your home.

- Buy a property that needs renovation if you can oversee the work. This lowers your purchase costs. You renovate over time and pay as you go.

- Plan on renovating at least the kitchen and bathrooms prior to your moving in, if you have rented the property.

- Figure on everything costing you more than planned unless you're a brilliant budgeter, fantastic negotiator, and you don't change your initial plans.

Summary of your information:
Example

Your monthly mortgage costs are	€1030
Your monthly insurance costs are	€90
Your monthly maintenance costs are	€95
Your total costs are	€1215

Your rent is	€950
The difference (profit or loss) is?	-€265
If this is a loss can you afford this?	Yes
Can you pay all costs if you've no tenant for 6 months?	No
Can you put 3 months of your mortgage and maintenance costs in a special rainy day account?	Yes

Yes means that you can feel comfortable about doing this deal. Put three months aside today and work on saving another three months.

If you live in the land of wishful thinking nothing bad will ever happen. Your home will always be rented, tenants will always pay and they will pay on time.

For the rest of us we plan. If you buy a retirement home and have tenants, make sure a few bad breaks will not force you into a fire sale or foreclosure.

Healthy Money Retirement Coaching

This is a twelve week group program to help you create a doable retirement plan.

Our goal working together is to find out where you want to live when you are retired and how much you will need. This is not a course where we discuss the ups and downs of the stock market. If you want to hear about the latest hot tip or hot financial product this course is not for you.

This fast track program helps you become an informed consumer. This means that when you work with your advisor you'll make better plans and investment choices.

When you work with your spouse or partner on creating a retirement plan you enhance your relationship and the process reduces stress. When I started out in my career in I was told; if you fail to plan, you plan to fail. This is still true today.

You'll be surprised at the income you actually need. For most of you it will be less than you think. Again this is truly life changing. Imagine what it feels like when you understand that you can retire five years early, or simply work because you want to.

On this program you're working with people who want an individual blueprint.

This is another low cost program because I want to change lives and work with positive people. This is a luxury that I have created for myself by using this program. Are you working with co-workers and clients that you enjoy working with? Financial freedom creates this lifestyle for you.

It wasn't always like this. When I was young and working as a sales person during the great Irish depression of the 1980's we worked with anyone who had a pulse.

If you're ready to plan for your retirement email retire@advisor-domain.com

10

MORE FOOTPRINTS IN THE SAND

If you've never read footprints in the sand you should.

I'll describe it in a minute.

When I first saw it I was with my wife in a local bookstore.

"Do you think that's us she asked?"

So of course to get the answer I had to read the poem. This short poem tells the story of a man talking to God about his life. God is explaining that he was with the man at all times. You see God said pointing to the footprints in the sand. He can see the footprints as far as the eye can see.

Along the beach there are two sets of footprints. The man points out to God the periods where there was only one set of footprints. "Oh that was where I was carrying you" says God.

"So do you think that's us?" asks my wife.

In any marriage there are times when one partner must carry the other, like one kid giving another a piggyback. I am hoping that these times in our marriage have been shared equally.

So why am I sharing this with you? It is simply to point out that the bad times like the good pass away. When you hit a rough spot say you become unemployed see this as being a challenge and not a way of life.

Sometimes I think that there is another possibility to footprints in the sand. What if God had said; "I let you be, you needed to work this out on your own?"

Extra Resources

Coaching Information:

I will be running 13 week (90 days) coaching group programs for anyone who wants to get on the fast track to goal accomplishment. You can go to our website www.advisordomain.com for more information. This will give you the bedrock on which to create the life of your dreams.

Fast track Debt Free 12 week coaching program

It does what it says on the tin.

This is a 12 week group coaching program done over the phone. We will use the entire goal setting tools, and fast track debt reduction techniques in a non judgemental setting.

You will move from being in debt to becoming debt free. Where you are will determine how fast you move and how many new actions that you need to take. We live in the day and we start with Daily doables. You will have a quarterly goal that you will accomplish.

By focussing on what can be done and actually getting this done you will change your life. Maybe you want to fast track debt freedom or possibly you are overwhelmed with debts. My philosophy based on my own life story is that you are not a debtor but a person with debts. This is a situation or life condition that can easily be changed.

It may take years but it is the journey that enriches you. Once you understand that you will become financially free all is changed. You will live in a whole new world. No longer will you be whipped around like a leaf in a storm. You will make your own choices no longer being swayed by the pied pipers of the guru world offering you wealth if only you buy their system.

At the end of 12 weeks you will have changed your internal compass, you will be grounded as a saver. You will be used to taking daily actions that move you towards a specific weekly goal. The weekly goals will help you achieve your monthly goal. And three months later you will achieve your quarterly goal.

This coaching is for people who want a fast kick start to being debt free. 12 weeks can change your life and put you on the path to creating a life that you can only dream of. Your dreams are no longer the pipe dreams of a wishful thinker but something that you can choose to achieve.

If you are ready to become debt free send an email to debtfree@ advisordomain.com I will let you know when the next classes commence. Each group is strictly limited to twelve students so you can get maximum benefit.

If you're ready to become debt free email debtfree@advisordomain.com

Retirement Coaching

This twelve week group program helps you create a healthy doable retirement plan.

Our goal working together is to find out where you want to live when you are retired and how much you will need. This is not a course where we discuss the ups and downs of the stock market. If you want to hear about the latest hot tip or hot financial product this course is not for you.

You will become an informed consumer. This means that when you work with your financial advisor you will make better plans and investment choices.

When you work with your spouse or partner on creating a retirement plan you enhance your relationship and the whole process reduces stress. When I started out in financial services I was told; if you fail to plan, you plan to fail. This is still true.

You'll be surprised at what income you actually need. For most of you it's less than you think. Again this is truly life changing. Imagine what it feels like when you understand that you can retire five years early, or simply work because you want to.

What you are doing on this program is creating an individual blueprint.

This is a low cost program because I want to change lives and work with positive people. This is a luxury that I have created by using this program. Are you working with people that you enjoy being with? Financial freedom creates new choices. It wasn't always like this. When I was young financial advisor during the great Irish depression of the 1980's we were told to work with anyone who had a pulse.

Are you ready to plan for your retirement? Email now retire@ advisordomain.com

LIFE EXPECTANCY CHART

Use this as a guide, it is not written in stone. Contact your financial advisor for more accurate information in your country.

Current Age	Expectation of Life
17	78.34
18	78.38
19	78.41
20	78.45
21	78.48
22	78.51
23	78.55
24	78.58
25	78.61
26	78.64
27	78.67
28	78.70
29	78.73

30	78.76
31	78.79
32	78.81
33	78.84
34	78.87
35	78.90
36	78.93
37	78.96
38	79.00
39	79.03
40	79.06

41	79.10
42	79.14
43	79.18
44	79.22
45	79.27
46	79.32
47	79.38

Current Age	Expectation of Life
48	79.43
49	79.50
50	79.57
51	79.64
52	79.72
53	79.81
54	79.90
55	80.01
56	80.12
57	80.24
58	80.37
59	80.52
60	80.67
61	80.84
62	81.02
63	81.21
64	81.42

You look for your age on the left. Beside this on the right is the age that you can expect to live to if you meet the average life expectancy.

For example:

You are 44 years old. You can expect to live to 79.22 years.

This information does not take into account, your lifestyle choices, nor does it take into account your gender. Women tend to live longer. Rich people also live longer. Smokers have a shorter life span. Life is good, become a non smoker!